MW00654906

"GOOD NEWS
FROM NEW ENGLAND"
by Edward Winslow

A volume in the series
Native Americans of the Northeast

Edited by
Colin Calloway
Jean M. O'Brien
Barry O'Connell

"GOOD NEWS
FROM NEW ENGLAND"
by Edward Winslow

A SCHOLARLY EDITION

Edited by
Kelly Wisecup

University of Massachusetts Press
Amherst and Boston

Copyright © 2014 by University of Massachusetts Press
All rights reserved
Printed in the United States of America

ISBN 978-1-62534-083-2 (paper); 082-5 (hardcover)

Designed by Dennis Anderson
Set in Adobe Jenson Pro by House of Equations, Inc.
Printed and bound by Sheridan Books, Inc.

Library of Congress Cataloging-in-Publication Data

Winslow, Edward, 1595–1655.
"Good news from New England" / by Edward Winslow ; edited by Kelly Wisecup. —
A scholarly edition.
pages cm. — (Native Americans of the Northeast)
Originally published: London : Printed by I. D. John Dawson for W. Bladen
and J. Bellamie, 1624.
Includes bibliographical references and index.
ISBN 978-1-62534-082-5 (hardcover : alk. paper) —
ISBN 978-1-62534-083-2 (pbk. : alk. paper)
1. Massachusetts—History—New Plymouth, 1620–1691.
2. Pilgrims (New Plymouth Colony)—Early works to 1800. [1. Indians of North
America—Massachusetts.]   I. Wisecup, Kelly, 1981–   II. Title.
F68.A66 2014
974.4'02—dc23
2014008144

British Library Cataloguing-in-Publication Data
A catalogue record for this book is available from the British Library.

CONTENTS

Section 3: Compromise and Conflict 143

ACKNOWLEDGMENTS

Thanks to Matt Cohen and Karen Ordahl Kupperman for their long-standing enthusiasm and support for this project and to Meghan Hughes Morton for sharing my interest in Winslow early on. Matt, Gabriel Cervantes, Alex Pettit, Dahlia Porter, and Cassander Smith provided helpful feedback on the introduction. In addition, Drew Lopenzina pointed me to Iroquois interpretations of arrows bound together, Ives Goddard commented on Winslow's spelling of Massachusett animate nouns, and Stephen Foster suggested references on John Bellamie. Elizabeth Veisz helped with research logistics and travels throughout Massachusetts during the summer of 2012. Thanks also to my graduate assistant, Erin Stalcup, for her expert work, and to the undergraduate students in my spring 2011 and 2013 ENGL 3912 courses, for helping me to consider how *Good News* is received in the classroom.

The staff at the John Carter Brown Library all provided immensely helpful feedback and resources during the summer of 2012, which made it a pleasure to do the research for this edition. Thanks especially to Val Andrews, Kim Nusco, Ken Ward, Leslie Tobias Olson, and John Minichiello. I'm also grateful to the Boston Public Library, the Massachusetts State Archives (especially Jennifer Fauxsmith), Pilgrim Hall Museum (especially Stephen O'Neill), Plimoth Plantation (especially Karin Goldstein and Bob Charlebois), the Tomaquag Indian Memorial Museum (especially Lorén Spears), the Massachusetts Historical Society, Old Bridgewater Historical Society, the Huntington Library, the British Library, the Newberry Library, the Library Company of Philadelphia, and the Rhode Island Historical Society.

At University of Massachusetts Press, I thank Clark Dougan, Bruce Wilcox, Carol Betsch, and the editors of the Native Americans of the Northeast series, Colin Calloway, Barry O'Connell, and Jean O'Brien, for their support of the edition and assistance along the way. Thanks as well to two anonymous reviewers, whose comments improved the edition.

The research for this edition was made possible by a fellowship from the John Carter Brown Library and by the Small Grant Program at the University of North Texas. Thanks also to the Department of English at UNT (especially to David Holdeman and Diana Holt) for supporting the edition with a Research Assistant Grant and with funds to offset the costs of reproducing images.

Finally, I thank Yale University Press for permission to reprint selections from *The Voyages of Giovanni da Verrazzano, 1524–1528*, ed. Lawrence C. Wroth (New Haven: Yale University Press, 1970), 135–36.

"GOOD NEWS
FROM NEW ENGLAND"
by Edward Winslow

INTRODUCTION

In the winter of 1622, word traveled throughout southern New England that the sachem, or leader, of the Pokanoket Wampanoags had fallen ill. Massasoit, or Ousemequin, as the sachem was known, had been unable to eat for several days, his tongue had swollen to such a size that he was unable to swallow, and he was losing his sight.[1] Massasoit's powahs, medical and religious specialists, were called to treat him. The powahs had studied medicinal remedies as well as rituals for appeasing the non-human powers who sent disease. In order to determine the spiritual cause of Massasoit's illness and thus to cure him, they probably smoked tobacco in order to enter into a state in which they were sensitive to supernatural powers, whether an impersonal force called manitou or the specific deities who were known to control illness. In addition, ritual movements and chants created a sacred space around the sachem's sickbed, a space from which the powahs could seek the aid of manitou. Women vigorously rubbed Massasoit's arms, perhaps in an attempt to restore his strength. Both the women and the powahs probably covered their bodies with black ashes, in order to signal their awareness that Massasoit was crossing the boundaries between life and death. It is likely that many Wampanoags joined the powahs' ceremonies, for healing rituals often involved the entire community.[2]

Massasoit's subjects in nearby Wampanoag communities and his allies also traveled to his village, at a place called Sowams (near what is now Bristol and Warren, R.I.), some of them from distances as great as one hundred miles. In this way, they followed Algonquian customs for

---

1. Massasoit is a title; Ousemequin seems to have been a given name. Winslow spelled the sachem's name Massassowat and Massasoyt. I use the contemporary spelling (Massasoit) throughout the introduction; the text of *Good News* and the related texts reproduce Winslow's spellings.

2. See Bragdon, *Native People*, 229, and Kupperman, *Indians and English*, 133.

enacting and solidifying friendship; they also displayed their loyalty to the sachem and their regard for his leadership. The numerous visitors also attested to the position of great respect that Massasoit held as the leader of many individual Wampanoag groups, each led by sachems who had put themselves under his protection and guidance. As one of his pnieses, or military advisors, a man named Hobbamock, noted, Massasoit was an ideal sachem, careful to respect others' opinions and not easily offended: "In anger and passion he was soon reclaimed, easy to be reconciled towards such as had offended him, ruled by reason in such measure, as he would not scorne the advice of mean men, and that he governed his men better with few strokes than others did with many."[3] The presence of powahs and allies alike made the sachem's sickbed a site where spiritual and political relationships were strengthened and negotiated.

One of these allies, an English colonist named Edward Winslow, also hoped to "profess" his friendship to Massasoit, and, like Massasoit's Algonquian visitors, he traveled the roughly forty miles from his village— which Native people called Patuxet but English colonists renamed Plimoth—to Sowams.[4] Winslow and another colonist, a gentleman named John Hamden, constituted the sole English delegation to Massasoit, for in 1622 Plimoth was one of only two small English settlements in the land colonial promoters referred to as New England. However, Winslow was no stranger to Sowams, for he had made the trip several times during the two years he had lived at Plimoth. He had slept in Massasoit's wetu (or house) with the sachem, his wife, and two "chief men" (probably pnieses), and he had often experienced Wampanoag hospitality, in the form of food and shelter, on these journeys.[5] Moreover, Winslow had been "necessarily called at some times to be with their [the Wampanoags'] sick," perhaps to provide medical care or to represent Plimoth's friendship.[6] By the time he joined the powahs, women, and other visitors, then, Winslow was at least partially familiar with acceptable protocol for showing respect to a powerful sachem and with the techniques that Wampanoag powahs employed

---

3. Winslow, *Good News*, 27.
4. Ibid., 26. On Plimoth's distance from Sowams, see Cushman, *Sermon Preached at Plimoth*, A3v (fifty miles), and Bradford, *Of Plymouth Plantation*, ed. Samuel Eliot Morison, 81 (forty miles).
5. *A Relation or Journal*, 45.
6. Winslow, *Good News*, 54.

to restore health to their patients. With the help of Hobbamock, who acted as a translator for the colonists in addition to serving Massasoit as his pniese, Winslow attempted to offer concrete signs of friendship: he expressed the colonists' desires for Massasoit's return to health, and he presented the sachem with a "confection of many comfortable conserves," probably a fruit-based medicinal concoction, which Winslow had brought from Plimoth.[7]

Massasoit accepted the conserves, and, to everyone's surprise, he was able to swallow the "juice" from the concoction.[8] Once he could see and speak again, Massasoit requested that Winslow recreate a broth the sachem had previously eaten at Plimoth. Winslow admitted that he was "unaccustomed and unacquainted in such businesses," or how to make the broth medicinal without familiar ingredients.[9] To compensate for his ignorance, Winslow turned to Algonquian medical practices, labor, and knowledge. He asked a Wampanoag woman to grind corn, or grains, ingredients that Algonquians frequently mixed with water and used for medicinal purposes.[10] He gathered sassafras roots, whose healing properties were well known to the Wampanoags, and strawberry leaves, possibly from plants that the Wampanoags had cultivated.[11] The broth slowly restored Massasoit's health: the sachem's sight improved, he had "three moderate stools," and he slept the night.[12] The next morning, Massasoit directed Winslow to provide the same medical care to other Wampanoag people who were ill.

Massasoit's requests not only ensured that he and his people would receive medical care from a man who was the colonists' primary diplomat to the Wampanoags but also incorporated Winslow into their networks

7. Ibid., 28.
8. Ibid.
9. Ibid., 29.
10. Roger Williams stated in 1643 that the Narragansetts effectively employed corn in medical concoctions, saying that "if the use of it were known and received in *England* (it is the opinion of some skillful in physic) it might save many thousand lives in *England*, occasioned by the binding nature of *English* wheat, the *Indian* Corn keeping the body in a constant moderate looseness." Williams, *Key into the Language*, 100. Winslow and Williams probably used "corn" to refer generally to grains rather than to maize in particular, since in the seventeenth century the term "corn" had a range of meanings.
11. See ibid., 98.
12. Winslow, *Good News*, 30.

of reciprocity and obligation. To accept Native generosity was, Massasoit reminded Winslow, to become "enmeshed in ties of obligation" that bound Winslow and the Wampanoags.[13] Indeed, Massasoit himself reciprocated Winslow's gift of medical care: he instructed Hobbamock to inform the colonist that the Massachusett people, who lived north of the Wampanoags, were planning to attack a second English colony, called Wessagusset. The Massachusetts also, Massasoit stated, planned to strike Plimoth before the colonists could counterattack.

By providing Winslow with information about the Massachusetts' alleged plot, Massasoit also reminded him of the alliance the colonists and Wampanoags had made in 1621, in which each group agreed to defend the other. Sharing the news of the Massachusetts' plan allowed Massasoit to confirm his status as a trustworthy ally of the colonists. After Winslow returned to Plimoth and relayed the sachem's statements, the colonists decided to act on the information by attacking the Massachusetts first. Plimoth's military leader, Myles Standish, chose a few colonists and traveled to Wessagusset, where they killed a total of seven Massachusett men, by trapping some of them in a room and by attacking others in a fight that took place outside the settlement. The colonists cut off the head of a Massachusett leader (probably a pniese) named Wituwamat and carried it back to Plimoth, where they mounted the dismembered head on a pole, as a "warning and terrour to all of that disposition," that is, to all who threatened the colonists.[14] In retaliation for the attack, the Massachusetts killed three Wessagusset men who had been living with them in order to obtain food. The attack had a dramatic effect on the Massachusetts and other area Native peoples: as Winslow explained, it "so terrified and amazed them, as in like manner they forsook their houses, running to and fro like men distracted, living in swamps and other desert places, and so brought manifold diseases amongst themselves, whereof very many are dead."[15]

English readers encountered the stories of Massasoit's illness and of the Plimoth colonists' attack in Winslow's printed account, a narrative

---

13. Bragdon, *Native People*, 132.
14. Winslow, *Good News*, 38.
15. Ibid., 46–47. On the colonists' attack, see also Salisbury, *Manitou and Providence*, 129–34.

called *Good News from New England,* which offered a history of events in New England between 1621 and 1623. Although Winslow wrote to justify the colonists' attack, he delayed a full representation of this violence by placing this account near the end of *Good News.* He first detailed the colonists' concerns that various tribes were conspiring to attack them (including the Narragansetts, the Massachusetts, and the Wampanoags), and he included colonists' observations of and encounters with Native peoples as evidence for these concerns. Meanwhile, his cure of Massasoit offered proof that the colonists had treated Native peoples with kindness and Christian charity. He also documented the colonists' often desperate attempts to obtain food, including their process of planting their fields and their travels along the coast to trade with Natives for corn. After finally recounting the attack on the Massachusetts and its aftermath, Winslow concluded *Good News* with a report on New England Natives' customs. Throughout the text, he attempted to assure readers, especially the colony's investors, who had financed the voyage to New England, that Plimoth would be a productive colony, one capable of repaying the colonists' debt with commodities such as corn and furs. He likewise sought to convince the colonists' religious leaders, who had remained behind in Leiden, the Netherlands, that the Plimoth colonists retained their Christian, English identities, as illustrated by their behavior and physical traits. This introduction establishes a number of contexts through which to examine *Good News:* literary genres of colonial travel and promotion; Winslow's experiences prior to traveling to the New World; and the histories of kidnapping, disease, and political tensions that shaped New England Natives' and colonists' responses to one another in the early 1620s.

Good News and Colonial Literatures

Good News includes many of the features that characterize early English colonial promotional writing, but it also complicates the genre in a number of ways. Winslow, like other colonial promoters, sought to convince readers of the colony's success before anyone was actually certain what its future would be. Unlike most colonial reports, however, *Good News* includes Winslow's acknowledgment of the colonists' reliance on Natives, for he drew on Native linguistic knowledge and his knowledge of Native peoples to represent New England. *Good News* offers a window into moments when neither colonists nor Natives were fully in control of events and their interpretations, but when multiple parties vied for power and when everyone struggled to understand the significance and meaning of their contacts with unfamiliar peoples.

The documents that comprise the literatures of early English transatlantic travel are as various as the experiences they recount: letters, natural histories (detailed descriptions of a place and its botanical, animal, and human life), official reports for investors, and true histories or relations (allegedly empirical reports of events that, as readers knew, were not always trustworthy). Although they were usually promotional in nature, nearly all English colonial reports before 1620 documented failed colonies or provided reconnaissance for settlements that were later abandoned (reports of Jamestown, in Virginia, offered the sole exception, but the colonists came close to abandoning the settlement at several points). Unable to celebrate actual accomplishments, colonial reports presented travelers' experiences and observations in the New World as signs of future possibilities. They imagined the resources that might be discovered or the colonies that would later be founded, and they likewise employed both descriptive language and lists that tabulated the New World's plenty in order to represent North America as possessing extensive resources and an environment that would support prosperity and health. Meanwhile, in England, colonial historians Richard Hakluyt and Samuel Purchas collected, excerpted, and published individual reports in extensive collections that provided evidence of England's imperial ventures. Yet colonial writers also had to struggle to maintain the optimistic model of peaceful, fruitful colonization and English superiority, for they included accounts of illness, starvation, and violent conflict with Native Americans that complicated imperial ideals.

For example, writing of Roanoke, in what is now North Carolina, Thomas Harriot emphasized the ease with which future settlers could make the colony profitable by noting that Roanoke Algonquians cultivated crops in the naturally fertile ground without extensive "husbanding."[16] John Smith took most of his observations of New England from a ship,

---

16. Harriot, *Brief and True Report*, 15.

but he nonetheless promised in 1614 that "besides the greatness of the Timber growing on them [islands], and the moderate temper of the air (for of twenty five, not any was sick, but two that were many years diseased before they went, notwithstanding our bad lodging and accidentall diet) who can but approve this a most excellent place, both for health & fertility?"[17] Harriot and Smith listed the many resources that Roanoke and New England, respectively, offered, from timber and fish to grain. In cases when colonists did not actually observe the resources they had been charged to discover, they imagined scenarios in which they would find those resources in the future. Ralph Lane, the military leader and eventually governor of the colony at Roanoke, explained in a report to Sir Walter Ralegh that although he had not located gold as Ralegh had instructed him to do, with sufficient supplies he "would" have followed a river where, he was certain, he would also have found gold.[18] In each of these cases, colonists presented their observations as evidence of future possibility rather than of present realities.[19] Yet they also included information that contradicted their optimistic predictions: Harriot and Lane explained that they departed Roanoke hastily, after failing to grow their own food and violent exchanges with the Roanoke Algonquians, and Smith admitted that he did not recommend settling parts of New England because of the large number of Natives already living there.

Native Americans played key roles in promotional narratives, for colonists described them as potential trading partners and converts for Protestantism, an especially important point for England given Spanish colonists' reports of their success converting Natives to Catholicism. Several English colonists reported that, after observing their technology and Protestant religious practices, Natives "feare[d] and love[d]" them.[20] They suggested that this love and fear indicated Natives' acknowledgment of English peoples' superiority; such episodes likewise reinforced claims

---

17. Smith, *Description of New England*, 10.

18. Lane, "An Account of the Particularities," 739.

19. Many scholars have examined the rhetorical strategies with which colonial writers familiarized their experiences and the New World for English readers as well as the techniques with which these writers promoted colonization. See, for just a few examples, Pagden, *European Encounters*; Fuller, *Voyages in Print*; Cheyfitz, *Poetics of Imperialism*; and Householder, *Inventing Americans*.

20. Harriot, *Brief and True Report*, 24; see also Rosier, *True Relation*, C1r.

that Natives would welcome settlers, their technologies, and their religion. As many accounts show, however, colonists often found themselves outwitted by Natives and reliant on Native people for food and their knowledge of local politics. For example, Lane heard Natives singing on one of his travels up a river in search of gold. At first, he believed the song to be one of welcome, but he quickly learned from his Roanoke guide that it was a signal to attack the Englishmen.[21]

Colonists also attempted to transform Native peoples into objects of study in moral—or cultural—histories of the New World. Many colonial reports included not just details about America's natural resources but also a "brief description of the nature and manners of the people of the country."[22] English writers followed the model of Spanish historians such as Gonzalo Fernández de Oviedo y Valdés and José de Acosta, who described the political systems, domestic practices, and religions of indigenous peoples in Spanish America. Although moral histories usually offered detailed accounts of Native life and culture, writers also attempted to assure readers that they had maintained their distance from the practices they observed: they separated moral histories from their travel narratives and removed rhetorical signs of cross-cultural interactions by employing a third-person point of view. For example, Acosta explained, "There is a kind of sorcerers amongst the Indians allowed by the Kings *Inguas,* which are as it were sooth-sayers"[23] and noted that "it was a pitiful thing to consider in what sort Satan held this people in his subjection, and doth many to this day."[24] Although Acosta related his own observations and considerations of the Native "sorcerers," his use of "there" and "it" removed any mention of the subject who observed Native religious practices.[25]

Winslow drew on the genres of the promotional report and moral history, even as *Good News* also exposes the fissures that appeared in those genres when writers had to revise their expectations of the Americas and strategies for engaging with Native peoples. Winslow's subtitle, "a true Relation of things very remarkable at the Plantation of *Plimoth* in New-England," signaled to readers that they could expect to find descriptions of

21. See Lane, "An Account of the Particularities," 741.
22. Harriot, *Brief and True Report,* 6.
23. Acosta, *Natural and Moral History,* 406.
24. Ibid., 357. See also Oviedo, "History of the West Indies," 181–82.
25. On moral histories, see Anthony Pagden, *Fall of Natural Man,* 149–57.

unusual or unexpected events from a first-person perspective.[26] Winslow
sought to present a narrative that would be viewed as trustworthy and
that promoted the productive, Christian community that, he claimed,
the colonists had established despite great obstacles. Moreover, by stating
that *Good News* would show "the wondrous providence and goodness of
God," he categorized his text as a "providence tale," a popular literary form
in which accounts of extraordinary happenings were interpreted as signs
of God's providence and authenticated with empirical evidence.[27] Providence tales related accounts not only of miracles and answered prayers
but also of divine judgments, often in the form of unusual and sensational
events, from monstrous births and plagues to appearances of dragons
and comets.[28] Although the Plimoth colonists struggled to survive the
winters and to find or grow food reliably, Winslow suggested that their
experiences offered signs of divine approval and thus of hope for the future. He also attempted to prove that the colonists' struggles were not due
to laziness, incompetence, or divine judgment but because the weather
was harsher and food more difficult to obtain than prior reports had
indicated. Finally, Winslow concluded *Good News* with a moral history
of Algonquian religious, medical, political, and domestic practices, which
he called a "Relation of such religious and civil Laws and Customs, as are
in practice amongst the *Indians*, adjoining to them at this day."[29]

But Winslow also included information in *Good News* that complicated his narrative of providential signs and future prosperity, not least
of which was the fact that the colonists preemptively attacked the Massachusetts. This decision not only undercut past claims that the colonists
lived in peace with New England Natives but also raised the question of
why the colonists had turned to violence to resolve the conflict with the
Massachusetts. Rather than insisting on the colonists' ability to subdue
or impress Native peoples, Winslow acknowledged their concerns regarding New England Algonquians' political, material, and military strength,
especially the fear that they would form an alliance and attack the colony. Furthermore, he represented moments when, far from presenting
English technology and religion as a superior model, he followed Natives'

---

26. Winslow, *Good News*, title page.
27. Ibid.
28. On providence tales, see Walsham, *Providence in Early Modern England*.
29. Winslow, *Good News*, title page.

commands and tried to act according to their customs. As we have already seen, Winslow imitated Native practices when making the decision to travel to Massasoit's bedside; he also conversed with Massasoit through the aid of a translator; he produced a healing broth, possibly a version of Algonquian medical remedies, by relying on the skill of a Wampanoag woman; and he obeyed Massasoit's directive to provide medical care to Wampanoags who were ill. Such actions threw into doubt colonists' past assurances that Natives would desire English practices and that English methods of agriculture, sustenance, and habitation could be reproduced in the New World.

Additionally, Winslow did not simply impose European literary forms and perspectives on his experiences but also drew from the linguistic and rhetorical strategies he observed in New England. *Good News* is a bilingual text that is written primarily in English and that not only includes Algonquian words, as other colonial reports did, but that also represents Algonquian linguistic practices.[30] More specifically, Winslow transcribed words in Massachusett pidgin, the contact language that the colonists and Natives employed to communicate. Pidgins were simplified versions of a language; they included a sufficient number of grammatical patterns for speakers to communicate. Yet while most pidgins strip out the animate and inanimate genders that Natives employed to distinguish among nouns, Winslow's spelling of Massachusett words is unique and suggests that he transcribed—and perhaps was aware of—Natives' linguistic practices for referencing animate entities.[31] Although most colonists used the now familiar terms "Massachusett" and "Narragansett" to refer both to the places where these people lived and to the people themselves, Winslow employed the suffix "-uck" when discussing tribes, such as the "Massacheuseucks," "Nanohiganneucks," and "Namascheucks." Contemporary studies of Massachusett linguistics note that plural animate nouns (such as the names for a people or tribe) were signaled by the suffix "-ak," which colonial writers sometimes represented as "-og," "-onk," or "-uonk."[32] Winslow's use of "-uck" at the end of names for New England

---

30. The Wampanoags and Massachusetts spoke a dialect known as Massachusett, also called Wampanoag today. See Goddard and Bragdon, *Native Writings in Massachusett*, xv.

31. On pidgins in colonial New England, see Goddard, "Use of Pidgins and Jargons."

32. See Goddard and Bragdon, *Native Writings in Massachusett*, 490–91.

peoples suggests that he attempted to represent the Massachusett suffix for a plural animate noun. He acknowledged in print Natives' linguistic signals for animate and inanimate entities, a move that suggests that he may also have had some understanding of the powers that Natives attributed to some non-human objects, such as tobacco.

Winslow's strategy of relating information about Native customs differed as well from the rhetorical practices previously established in moral histories. In contrast to the distancing, non-narrative strategies that characterized most colonial moral histories, *Good News* highlighted the oral exchanges in which Winslow had obtained information. For example, in his description of Natives' cultural practices, Winslow foregrounded his informants' voices by repeating the phrase "they say."[33] In this way, the moral history made visible the connections between the information in *Good News* and his Native sources, and it represented these sources as speakers rather than as objects.

Finally, Winslow included in the moral history a printed marginal note with information about Kiehtan, one of the Wampanoags' deities, in which he observed: "The meaning of the word Kiehtan, I think hath reference to Antiquity, for *Chise* is an old man, and *Kiehchise* a man that exceedeth in age."[34] Winslow's knowledge of Massachusett linguistics and religious beliefs, as displayed in the note, is made all the more interesting by the fact that he had stated only two years earlier that the Natives had no religion, in a promotional report of Plimoth probably written by Winslow and another colonist, William Bradford.[35] Winslow's moral history thus not only corrected his previous, mistaken assumptions but also made clear the links between exchanges with Native peoples and the content of *Good News*.

As these examples suggest, *Good News* is not a representation of colonial experiences alone, nor did Winslow's perspective as an English colonist and a religious dissenter entirely determine how he described events and people in New England. This is the case for several reasons.

---

33. See Winslow, *Good News*, 52–53.
34. Ibid., 52.
35. See *Relation or Journal*, 61. Bradford was chosen as Plimoth's second governor in 1621, a position he would hold for much of his life. In 1620, both Bradford and Winslow were young men, and the *Relation* represents their first attempts to describe and to promote the colony.

First, Winslow needed to include Natives' perspectives and voices in order to provide "good news" from the New World, to show, for example, that the colonists had established productive cross-cultural relations and secured their participation in trading networks. He also sought to quiet critics with evidence that the colonists had not become excessively violent, namely, that they did not kill the Massachusett men without concrete foreknowledge of a plan to attack Plimoth. Furthermore, Native peoples were necessary to show that the colonists were bringing "good news" to New England, that is, that they had attempted to bring God's Word and the gospel to Algonquians. Winslow also suggested that, despite the threat of attacks from violent Natives, he could present the "good news" that the colonists had survived.

Second, Winslow did not always control how information circulated or how people in New England responded to or interpreted events. Indeed, Massasoit and other Native peoples alternately determined, complicated, and assisted many of the colonists' actions and decisions, including what they knew of events and how they interpreted Natives' actions. As a consequence, *Good News* provides a fascinating glimpse into the strategies that Natives in New England employed to interpret the newcomers' intentions, strategies the Wampanoags had been employing for several decades to engage with Europeans before the Plimoth colonists arrived. The book likewise illuminates the ways in which Winslow and other colonists attempted to interpret Natives' actions.

The publication of *Good News* in London was part of this struggle to decipher events in New England and to ensure that the news about Plimoth was indeed perceived as "good." In a "brief Relation" added to the second edition (also published in 1624), Winslow explained that the Plimoth colonists had received news of a coordinated attack by Powhatan people on English colonists from a ship that sailed from Virginia to New England.[36] In 1622, Powhatans had walked unarmed into colonial villages, much as they had done for the past fifteen years; they then seized and

---

36. In the second 1624 edition, the title page was reset to include the line "Whereunto is added by him a brief Relation of a credible intelligence of the present estate of Virginia," and the "brief Relation" was inserted following the text of *Good News*. I discuss the two 1624 editions of *Good News* in detail below, in the introduction section titled "Note on the Text."

used colonists' own weapons against them, killing over three hundred people. *Good News*'s title page states that Winslow wrote the relation and added it at the "earnest entreaty of some of my much respected friends."[37] It is possible that publisher John Bellamie was also behind the decision to reprint *Good News* with the relation, perhaps in order to increase sales of the book.[38] English readers were already accustomed to reading salacious reports of violence, cannibalism, and exotic practices from the Americas written by Spanish and French colonists; accounts of violence—whether it took place in the New or Old World—were bestsellers. Furthermore, news of preemptive *Native* violence in Virginia could justify preemptive *colonial* violence in New England by suggesting that the Plimoth colonists were right to take action against the Massachusetts before they became victims of an attack like the one in Virginia. Adding the relation thus included the violence in New England in a larger story about Native attacks on colonists in North America.

Few contemporary editors of Winslow's text have taken account of the fact that the relation about violence in Virginia was added only in a second edition.[39] Moreover, Native actions, communications, and influences have not formed part of the context in which *Good News* is usually read. In the case of *Good News*, colonial writers and U.S. American editors excerpted and paraphrased the text in order to support their views of New England colonization, cross-cultural relations, and the history of the United States. Subsequent editions of Winslow's text can be grouped into two categories: seventeenth-century adaptations and nineteenth-century reproductions, which twentieth-century versions replicate. In 1624, John

37. Winslow, *Good News*, brief Relation.

38. By 1624, John Bellamie had already published several texts on English colonization, including Robert Cushman's sermon preached at Plimoth and the 1622 *A Relation or Journal of the Beginning and Proceedings of the English Plantation Settled at Plimoth in New England*, probably written by Winslow and Bradford. Bellamie continued to publish books on New England, including publications from Massachusetts Bay Colony, some of John Eliot's tracts, and Winslow's later writings against colonist Samuel Gorton. He likewise published religious texts, including the first English editions of the Separatist minister John Robinson's writings and "Puritan polemics and theological commentaries." Indeed, Bellamie was an ideal publisher for the Plimoth colonists, for he had joined a Separatist congregation in 1616. Like Winslow, he supported the Puritans in the English Civil War, in which he participated as a publisher, soldier, and author. See Rostenberg, "New World," 21–23 (quotation on 21).

39. As discussed below, Jack Dempsey's 2001 edition is an exception.

Smith excerpted and summarized Winslow's account in the sixth book of his *Generall History of Virginia, New England, & the Summer Isles*.[40] Just a year later, in 1625, the clergyman and colonial promoter Samuel Purchas included an edited version of *Good News* in a volume of his collection of travel narratives, *Purchas his Pilgrims*.[41] He cut the last few pages of *Good News*, in which Winslow explained that hard work was required for future colonists to sustain themselves. In 1677, the Puritan minister Increase Mather excerpted parts of *Good News* in his history of the New England colonies. He placed the Plimoth colonists' first years in America in a narrative of hostilities that culminated in 1675 in King Philip's War, a conflict between multiple, united tribes and the colonies. Mather combined parts of *Good News* with an earlier text to which Winslow had contributed, *A Relation or Journal of the Beginning and Proceedings of the English Plantation Setled at Plimouth in New England* (often known as *Mourt's Relation*). He included these texts with other colonial reports under a new title: *A Relation of the Troubles which have happened in New-England, By reason of the Indians there. From the Year 1614 to the Year 1675. Wherein the frequent Conspiracies of the Indians to cut off the English, and the wonderful providence of God, in disappointing their devices, is declared. Together with an Historical Discourse concerning the Prevalency of Prayer shewing that New Englands late deliverance from the Rage of the Heathen is an eminent Answer of Prayer.* As this long title suggests, the minister made *Good News* part of a history that showed how colonists received providential redemption from Native Americans' violent attacks. Mather glossed over the colonists' own attack on the Massachusetts, noting only that there were "several skirmishes with the Indians."[42]

Interest in *Good News* seems to have faded in the eighteenth century, but in the nineteenth century, editors began to reissue Winslow's text and to redefine it as a founding text of the American nation and its history. In this way, they presented the Plimoth colonists as proto-U.S. Americans, despite the fact that this identity was unimaginable to the colonists. Editors reproduced Winslow's text in histories of the Pilgrims, as the Plimoth colonists were by then called. Moreover, they included the

---

40. See Smith, *General History* (1624), 236–43.
41. See Purchas, *Purchas His Pilgrims*, 1853–71.
42. See Mather, *Relation of the Troubles*, 19.

second edition's relation on Virginia without noting that it was not in-cluded in the first 1624 edition. In 1826, Thomas Prince summarized *Good News* in his *Chronological History of New-England: in the Form of Annals.* A few years later, in 1841, Alexander Young included Winslow's text in his *Chronicles of the Pilgrim Fathers of the Colony of Plymouth, from 1602–1625.* Young presented his *Chronicles* as the "first book of our history."[43] He made several substantial changes to the 1624 edition of Winslow's text by adding chapter headings and dates that are not in the original text. In addition, he relocated the "brief Relation" about Virginia from the end of the text, where it appeared in 1624, to the beginning of the text, follow-ing the "To the Reader" section. Young's edition thus foregrounded the Powhatans' attack on the Jamestown colonists over Winslow's account of the Plimoth colonists' attack on the Massachusetts.[44] Finally, in 1897, Edward Arber reproduced *Good News* in *The Story of the Pilgrim Fathers, 1606–1623, AD; as told by Themselves, their Friends, and their Enemies.* Arber included the first edition title page and added annotations and headings, and he placed the "briefe Relation" at the end of the text.[45]

A 1996 edition published by Applewood Books includes Young's chap-ter headings and dates as well as his arrangement of the "brief Relation" about the attack at Jamestown. Moreover, Applewood relocates Win-slow's printed marginal note about Native religious practices to endnotes. In contrast to most contemporary editions, Jack Dempsey's 2001 edition of *Good News* returns to a 1624 copy text, although Dempsey does not account for the two editions of *Good News* issued in 1624. Dempsey's introduction and his selections of supplementary materials focus on the colonists' attack on the Massachusetts, for he aims to show that the colonists attempted to carry out "radical programmatic reform of New England's early [Native] ways," a plan that included "conquest, conversion, and (profitable) commerce."[46]

Good News does not appear in the Bedford, Heath, or Norton antholo-gies of American literature. Instead, selections from William Bradford's *Of Plymouth Plantation* and Thomas Morton's 1637 critique of Plimoth

43. Young, *Chronicles of the Pilgrim Fathers,* x.
44. See ibid., 270–375.
45. Arber, *Story of the Pilgrim Fathers,* 509–600.
46. Dempsey, introduction to *Good News from New England,* xx.

colony, *New English Canaan*, represent early New England colonial writing. Such excerpts highlight the Plimoth colonists' conflicts with both
Native peoples and with colonists such as Morton. Similarly, an excerpt
from *Mourt's Relation* in the 2011 edition of the *Norton Anthology of American Literature* emphasizes the colonists' fear of New England Natives.
The *Broadview Anthology of Seventeenth-Century Prose* excerpts only
Winslow's moral history.[47]

Thus if between 1621 and 1623 the Wampanoags and colonists recognized that their stories were interconnected and that they needed one
another to survive, editors of Winslow's text forgot or obscured the fact
that *Good News* described colonists' engagement with and reliance on
Native American peoples, practices, and communications and, likewise,
Natives' investigation of some English linguistic, religious, and medical
practices. Instead, *Good News* was incorporated into an optimistic, teleo-
logical history of colonization and of intercultural conflict in New England, a history that continues to influence editions and analyses of the text
in the twenty-first century.

By contrast, this edition restores *Good News* to the seventeenth-
century circumstances in which it was produced and consumed, including the contexts of Native actions and knowledge.[48] The introduction and
related texts make it possible to read *Good News* in the context not only
of early English colonization but also of Native responses to colonization.
Without forgetting the violence and dispossession that characterized
Europeans' exploration of and settlement in the New World, the edition illuminates the mutual uncertainty that characterized cross-cultural
encounters in the early 1620s, and it highlights the strategies with which
some colonists and Natives made alliances and attempted to live together.
This introduction attends to the multiple voices and knowledge systems
that contributed to *Good News*: both the knowledge and practices that
Natives employed as they observed, incorporated, or rejected the European newcomers and the ideas and beliefs that colonists imported from

---

47. See Bradford and Winslow, "From Mourt's Relation," 71–75, and Winslow, *Good
News (excerpt): Religion and Customs*, 236–41.

48. For scholarship that attends to the Native presence in or influence on colonial
texts, see Donohue, *Bradford's Indian Book*; Jehlen, "History Before the Fact"; White,
"Invisible Tagkanysough"; Whitehead, "*Discoverie* as enchanted text" and "*Discoverie* as
ethnological text"; and Wisecup, *Medical Encounters*, esp. the introduction.

Europe. The related texts represent some of the experiences that shaped Natives' and colonists' responses to one another. They also depict moments when many people in New England—colonists, Wampanoags, Narragansetts, and Massachusetts—were unsure of the outcome of cross-cultural relations. These texts make it possible to read *Good News* in light of colonial and Native concerns of the early seventeenth century, rather than in the context of later cross-cultural conflicts, such as King Philip's War, or of Plimoth's status as one of the first successful English colonies. At the same time, as discussed in the "Note on the Text" below, this edition returns to a 1624 copy text, and it attends to the variations in the two 1624 editions.

Edward Winslow: Cross-Cultural Diplomat

Winslow was an ideal candidate to write Plimoth's history and to defend the colonists' attack on the Massachusetts. As colonial diplomat and defender, Winslow combined an ongoing interest in and desire for information about New England Native peoples with a commitment to English colonization and colonial authority. Moreover, his education and livelihood before traveling to New England supplied him with experiences and knowledge that could have served as a foundation for his engagement with Native peoples. He was born in Droitwich (in northern England) in 1595 to Magdalen Ollyver and Edward Winslow, Sr., a farmer and saltmaker with aspirations to raise his status to that of a gentleman.[49] The younger Winslow received an education at the King's School of Worcester Cathedral between 1606 and 1611, where students acquired a knowledge of Latin and the *Book of Common Prayer*, the Church of England's guide to prayer and communion that many of Winslow's fellow Separatists later argued should be removed from religious practice altogether.

After his formal education, Winslow worked as an apprentice in London for printer John Beale. In the course of this work, he would have encountered a variety of popular texts, including reports of the New World and its peoples. Beale printed many sermons and devotional guides as well as several plays, accounts of murders, and travel narratives

---

49. Travers, "Winslow, Edward (1595–1655)."

of Guiana and Virginia during Winslow's apprenticeship.[50] Winslow would have also assisted in the printing of Gervase Markham's *The Complete English Huswife*, a domestic manual that included a lengthy home medical guide. In addition, Beale published Francis Bacon's *Essays*, which advocated experience and observation as the foundations of knowledge. Winslow could thus have been familiar with travelers' descriptions of Native peoples' medicinal knowledge and expertise; at the same time, he would have known of the value that many readers had begun to give to experiential (rather than textual) knowledge.[51]

Winslow was bound to Beale in 1613 for a term of eight years, but he broke or was released early from his apprenticeship, although the means by which he left are not known.[52] By 1617, he had joined a group of English religious dissenters, called Separatists, in Leiden, the Netherlands. The Separatists had broken from the Church of England because they felt it had strayed too far from the "invisible church" of godly saints; they sought instead to establish a church of "Professing Christians" who were joined by "voluntary agreements or covenants made among themselves."[53] When the Separatists made plans to establish a colony in the New World, Winslow agreed to travel to America as both settler and investor, meaning that he personally contributed to the funding for the journey and supplies and that he would receive a return on his investment once the colony became profitable.[54] By the time he wrote *Good News*, then, Winslow probably had some experience negotiating with the colonists' London

---

50. Beale's New World publications during this period include Robert Harcourt, *A Relation of a Voyage to Guiana, Describing the Climate, Situation, Fertility, Provisions and Commodities of that Country . . . Together with the manners, customs, behaviours, and dispositions of the people* (London, 1613), and Ralph Hamor, *A true discourse of the present estate of Virginia and the success of the affairs there till the 18 of June. 1614 . . . Written by Ralph Hamor the younger, late secretary in that colony* (London, 1615).

51. On Winslow's early life, see Wolkins, "Edward Winslow (O.V. 1606–11)," 235–66; and Bangs, *Pilgrim Edward Winslow*, chap. 1.

52. See Bangs, *Pilgrim Edward Winslow*, 3–4.

53. Morgan, *Visible Saints*, 26.

54. The colonists had permission to settle within the Virginia Company's patent, but they landed too far north to do so. It is possible that the colonists had permission from Ferdinando Gorges to settle in New England; they certainly had information from Thomas Dermer regarding the depopulation of Patuxet, making it possible that they traveled to New England in hopes of settling in a place where they would not meet with Native opposition. See Salisbury, *Manitou and Providence*, 109. On Winslow and others as both investors (or Adventurers) and colonists, see ibid., 111–12.

investors, experience that would have served him well in 1623 when he needed to defend the colonists' actions to this audience.

But prior knowledge did not provide Winslow with all the information he needed in New England, for he also had to adapt to the circumstances and peoples he encountered in the New World. He may have been willing to imitate Native practices because he recognized that the colonists could not survive their first years in New England if they simply tried to replicate familiar methods of healing, finding food, and engaging with other people. Winslow, and the other colonists as well, had to modify the preconceived ideas they had of Natives, ideas based on travelers' accounts of brief trading encounters or observations made from ships' decks. Indeed, many of these preconceptions did not serve the colonists well: William Bradford reported that they expected the Natives to torture and eat them, writing that the Natives would "torment men in the most bloody manner that may be; flaying some alive with the shells of fishes, cutting off the members and joints of others piecemeal and broiling on the coals, eat the collops of their flesh in their sight whilst they live, with other cruelties horrible to be related."[55] Bradford's expectations were probably founded on earlier Spanish, Italian, and French accounts of cannibalism rather than on firsthand reports from New England.[56] The colonists certainly drew on prior knowledge in their encounters with New England Algonquians, but they also had to improvise in situations for which they had no precedent. Similarly, New England Algonquians had some knowledge of European colonists, but they also found themselves in unfamiliar situations after the Plimoth colonists arrived in 1620. Natives and colonists alike struggled to ascertain the motives and nature of the new people they met, and they all attempted to interact with unfamiliar people in ways that improved their own power and influence.

Captives and Emissaries

Much of the knowledge that New England Natives and English colonists had of one another in 1620 circulated through indigenous captives

---

55. Bradford, *Of Plymouth Plantation*, 26.

56. Accounts by Amerigo Vespucci and John de Lery contained descriptions of cannibals that may have influenced Bradford's predictions. See Vespucci, *Letters*, and de Lery, *History of a Voyage*.

kidnapped by explorers and forcibly taken to England. There, they acted
as representatives of their people and collected information about Europe
and its peoples. Although most captives never returned home, those who
did used their experiences as a foundation on which to make decisions
about how to respond to European colonists. Algonquians in southern
New England made contact with Europeans as early as 1524, when the
Italian explorer Giovanni da Verrazzano sailed along the coast.[57] Such
contacts usually occurred during the summer, when Native peoples were
collecting resources along the coasts and working in fishing camps. These
temporary camps were bustling centers, for men and women worked to
harvest seasonally available foods such as fish and summer plants before
returning to more permanent villages for the winter months. Although
Wampanoag, Massachusett, Abenaki, and Narragansett peoples established trading relations with Europeans, primarily French and Dutch
travelers, in the early seventeenth century, these relations were unstable
from the beginning, given that Europeans began to kidnap Native peoples
as early as Verrazzano's voyages (see the related texts in section 1).

In the late sixteenth and early seventeenth centuries, England lagged
behind Spain, France, and Portugal when it came to New World ventures
and colonies, but English colonists quickly established captive taking
as a regular practice.[58] On his voyage to the Arctic in 1576, Sir Martin
Frobisher captured an Inuit man, woman, and child; he brought them
back to London, where they died, either from illnesses contracted on
their voyage or in the city, or from wounds sustained when the explorers
kidnapped and violently restrained them.[59] (Figure 1) Less than a decade
later, in 1584, two Roanoke Algonquian men, Wanchese and Manteo, accompanied colonists on a voyage from their home in Ossomocomuck

---

57. Early contacts between Europeans and New England Algonquians also occurred
during Samuel de Champlain's travels to "Cape St. Louis," which English colonists would
name Plimoth, in 1605. In 1609, the Dutch explorer Henry Hudson traveled along the
New England coast; in 1614, Adriaen Block traveled to Buzzards Bay, Long Island, and the
Connecticut River, where he later established Dutch trading networks. See Champlain,
Works of Samuel de Champlain, and Jameson, ed., *Narratives of New Netherland*.

58. Spanish explorers initiated the practice of taking captives as early as Columbus's
voyages to the Caribbean. On the connection between English and Spanish practices of
taking captives, see Householder, *Inventing America*, 147. On Natives who traveled to
Europe as captives, see Vaughan, *Transatlantic Encounters*, and Weaver, "Red Atlantic."

59. On Frobisher's captives, see Cheshire, Waldron, Quinn, and Quinn, "Frobisher's
Eskimos."

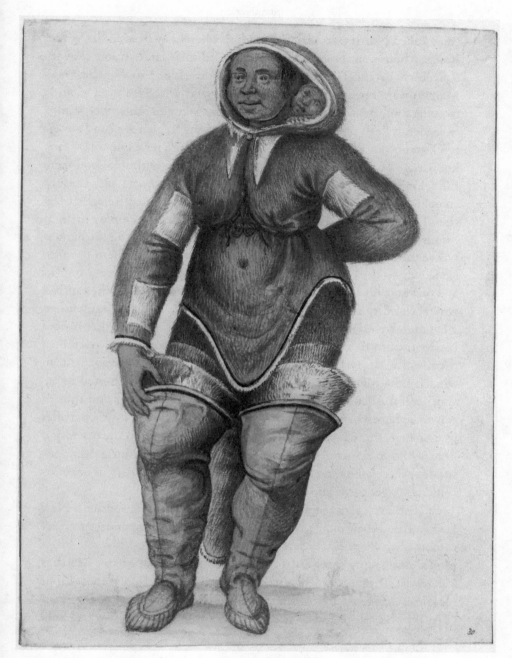

Figure 1. John White, *Arnaq and Nutaaq, Inuit from Frobisher Bay* (1585–1593). © Trustees of the British Museum.

(now called North Carolina) to London, where they lived in Sir Walter Ralegh's house on the Strand and discussed their land's resources with Ralegh's assistant Thomas Harriot. It is possible that Wanchese and Manteo were not captives but diplomats who were sent on a mission to collect information about the English by Wingina, their werowance, or leader. Ralegh probably used their testimony to plan a second voyage to Ossomocomuck, in 1586, and Wingina seems to have employed their knowledge of Englishmen to make his decision to withhold food from the colonists, thus hastening their departure. In the seventeenth century, colonial investors such as Ferdinando Gorges continued Ralegh's practice of attempting to teach Native men English and to employ them as resources about America. Gorges instructed the explorers on the numerous ventures he financed to return with Native captives, whom he questioned about the resources and geography of their land in order to plan and promote his future ventures. Gorges's men took most of the captives who traveled to England between 1600 and 1620, and they established what came to be fairly common strategies for taking captives: they invited Native men to their ship with the promise of trade and then restrained them as the ship left. Writing of a 1605 voyage made to Wabanaki (in what is now Maine), James Rosier explained that he attempted to assure several Abenaki men of the colonists' good intentions and thus to convince them to come to the Englishmen's boat by showing "them trifles to exchange, thinking thereby to have banished fear from the other, and drawn him to return: but when we could not, we used little delay, but suddenly laid hands upon them. And it was as much as five or six of us could do to get them into the light horseman."[60]

English explorers employed these same strategies in southern New England, and their tactics convinced a number of Wampanoags to limit contact with English travelers. In 1614, a captain named Thomas Hunt took about twenty captives from communities at Noepe (now Martha's Vineyard), Patuxet, and Nemasket.[61] As Gorges later reported, Hunt took these captives "by treachery, and under pretence of friendship enticed into his Ship, and as it came afterwards to be known, had sold

60. Rosier, *True Relation*, C4v.
61. On Hunt's actions, see *Relation or Journal*, 35, and Gorges, "Description of New England," 20.

them to the *Spaniards* in the streights of *Gibraltar*."[62] Colonists who attempted to trade with Wampanoag peoples after Hunt's voyage found
that "the *Savages* from thence contracted so great an animosity toward the
English, that Captain *Hobson* was constrained to return without doing any
thing."[63] Hunt's actions were still a recent memory among Wampanoag
communities when the colonists arrived at Plimoth. They reported in
Mourt's Relation that a woman came to meet them during one of their
exploratory trips because she had never before seen English people. Yet,
when she met the colonists, the woman "could not behold us without
breaking forth into great passion, weeping and crying excessively."[64] When
they inquired into the reason for her weeping, the colonists found that
her three sons had been captured by Hunt. They attempted to assure her
that not all Englishmen behaved as Hunt had and that "all the English
that heard of it condemned him"; in an attempt to compensate for Hunt's
actions, they gave her some "small trifles."[65]

Although the Native captives who traveled to London and other parts
of Europe did not control their routes or whether they would return to
their homelands, they did sometimes influence Europeans' actions and
perspectives in ways that advanced their own or their peoples' goals. In
1611, a Martha's Vineyard Wampanoag sachem, Epenow, was kidnapped by
Captain Edward Harlow and taken to London, where Gorges attempted
to employ him as an expert on New England's resources. Gorges noted
that Epenow was displayed to London crowds, and he commented that
Epenow had "learned so much *English* as to bid those that wondered at
him, welcome, welcome."[66] Whatever his thoughts while he was displayed
in England, Epenow seems to have used his knowledge of English desires
in order to accelerate his 1614 return voyage to Martha's Vineyard: aware
of the English curiosity about New World resources, Epenow informed
Gorges of the "commodities" that could be found near his island.[67] Once
he returned to Martha's Vineyard with Gorges's men, however, Epenow

---

62. Gorges, "Description of New England," 20.
63. Ibid. Nicholas Hobson worked for Gorges.
64. *Relation or Journal*, 50. The colonists were at Cummaquid (now Barnstable,
Mass.)
65. Ibid.
66. Gorges, *Briefe Narration*, 13.
67. Ibid., 14.

did not welcome the English. Instead, he orchestrated his escape by instructing his fellow Wampanoags to come to the ship with their weapons hidden. The English captain believed that the Wampanoags came to trade, but once they arrived, Epenow "flip[ped] himself over board, and although he were taken hold of by one of the company, yet being a strong and heavy Man, could not be stayed, and was no sooner in the water, but the Natives sent such a shower of arrows, and came withal desperately so near the Ship."[68] Epenow seems to have warned the Wampanoags of the English travelers' desire for captives and for information about New England's resources; he also seems to have determined to repel any future overtures from the English. In 1620, when Thomas Dermer, another of Gorges's men, returned to New England, Epenow led an attack on him.[69] Interestingly, Epenow spoke with Dermer before the attack, and Dermer reported that Epenow "laughed at his own escape."[70] The meaning of Epenow's laughter is not clear: did he find his escape amusing? Did he enjoy the Englishmen's failure? Was his laughter ironic, an indication of his knowledge of English plans for colonization and exploration? Epenow continued to correctly anticipate English tactics and actions, for he "questioned him [Dermer] about me [Gorges] and all he knew belonged unto me, conceived he was come on purpose to betray him, and conspired with some of his fellows to take the Captain."[71] Epenow thus escaped not only Gorges's men but also Gorges's attempts to employ him to promote colonial voyages. Instead, the sachem used his knowledge of English colonial designs to control travelers' access to his people and their resources.

One of Thomas Hunt's captives, a Patuxet man known as Tisquantum (also called Squanto), likewise influenced both English and Wampanoag peoples by applying the knowledge he gained on transatlantic voyages. At some point after his kidnapping by Hunt in 1614, Tisquantum maneuvered out of or was removed from Hunt's possession. Accounts of Tisquantum's travels throughout Europe are fragmentary at best: in one story, Spanish priests realized that the men about to be sold as slaves were Native

68. Ibid., 16.
69. Neal Salisbury suggests that Epenow may have been retaliating for the death of several Pokanoket Wampanoags, who had recently been shot without provocation by English sailors. See Salisbury, *Manitou and Providence,* 108.
70. Gorges, *Briefe Narration,* 20.
71. Ibid.

Americans and rescued some of them on the basis of the argument that their souls had to be saved first. In another report, Tisquantum was purchased by an English merchant.[72] By 1617, he was living in England, in the household of John Slanie (or Slany), who was treasurer of the Newfoundland Company. After traveling to Newfoundland, probably with English fishermen, Tisquantum returned to London with Thomas Dermer. Like Epenow, Tisquantum probably provided Gorges with information about the resources, geography, and peoples in his homeland. Although Gorges had been instructing his men to take Native captives for nearly two decades by the time he met Tisquantum, he seems to have hoped that he had finally found a captive who would help him realize his plans. In particular, Gorges wanted to use Tisquantum's knowledge of both English and Algonquian languages to assist his ventures by easing tense relations with indigenous peoples in New England, thus countering French success in establishing trade networks in the region. But Hunt's actions and the long history of kidnapping in New England compromised Gorges's plans, for Tisquantum's return with Dermer was met by Epenow's attack. The Wampanoags took Tisquantum captive, and by the time the Plimoth colonists had crossed the Atlantic, Tisquantum was living at Sowams. Like Gorges, Massasoit must also have decided that Tisquantum's knowledge of English language and culture could be useful; in 1621, he sent Tisquantum to serve as one of the colonists' translators at Plimoth, ironically on the same site where his village had formerly been located.

Tisquantum employed his knowledge of the English and of his own people to improve his status and to make himself such a valuable "instrument" to the colonists that, although they complained that they could not trust him, they also admitted that they could not function without him.[73] He acted as their guide on exploratory and trading ventures, and he served as translator in various exchanges with Algonquian people, exchanges the colonists desperately needed to obtain food for themselves and furs for investors. But Tisquantum also acted in ways that went counter to the colonists' purposes: for example, he once attempted to convince them that

---

72. Increase Mather suggested that Spanish priests took the captives to "nurture them in the Popish Religion." See Mather, *Relation of the Troubles*, 2. For other accounts of Tisquantum's captivity, see *Relation or Journal*, 35, and Pratt.

73. Winslow, *Good News*, 8.

Massasoit was preparing to attack them. During one of the colonists' journeys to trade with the Massachusetts, a member of Tisquantum's family
came "running to certain of our people that were from home with all eagerness, having his face wounded, and the blood still fresh on the same,
calling to them to repair home, oft looking behind him, as if some others
had him in chase."[74] The man stated that Massasoit had joined the Narragansetts and planned to attack the colonists while the trading party
was away. However, Hobbamock contradicted this message by insisting
that Massasoit would not undertake a course of war against his allies,
especially not without first consulting with Hobbamock and other pnieses. As the colonists discovered, the news of the attack was one of several
elaborate rumors Tisquantum circulated, for he also sent word that the
colonists were planning to attack the Wampanoags. Such claims were so
compelling that Wampanoag people considered leaving Massasoit's guidance and giving trust and tribute to Tisquantum to secure his protection.

Both Massasoit and the Plimoth colony leaders found Tisquantum's
behavior infuriating. Massasoit insisted that Tisquantum be turned over
to him for execution as a traitor, and Plimoth governor William Bradford
"sharply reproved" Tisquantum,[75] complaining that he "sought his own
ends, and played his own game, by putting the Indians in fear, and draw-
ing gifts from them to enrich himself."[76] Yet the colonists also refused to
hand Tisquantum over to Massasoit, and they continued to rely on his
geographic, political, and linguistic skills until his death from illness during the winter of 1622–23. Tisquantum's experiences endowed him with
immensely valuable skills and knowledge, yet these qualities also isolated
him from both colonists and other Natives. His ability to heighten tensions with reports of impending attacks also illuminates the uncertainty
felt by both Wampanoag and English people about one another.

Disease and Disorder

In 1614, the same year Tisquantum was captured, John Smith surveyed New England's coast and commented that the large population
of Algonquian peoples—up to three thousand in some places, Smith

---

74. Ibid., 6.
75. Ibid., 8.
76. Bradford, *Of Plymouth Plantation*, 99.

noted—would deter potential colonists. But six years later, Tisquantum's village was deserted, and most of his people, who had formerly numbered about 2,000, were dead. What Tisquantum missed during his enforced travels was one of the most traumatic events to occur in New England in the early seventeenth century. Beginning around 1616, virulent epidemics broke out, affecting great numbers of Massachusett and Wampanoag peoples, but largely sparing the Narragansetts and inland peoples. The epidemics seemed to infect people with access to French trading routes or those who came into contact with Native peoples who, like the Massachusetts, traded frequently with the French.[77] Scholars estimate that the epidemics reduced populations of Algonquian peoples along the New England coast by as much as ninety percent.[78] Villages that had hundreds and sometimes thousands of occupants before the illnesses were reduced to a few dozen people; some villages, like Patuxet, all but disappeared, with survivors joining other groups. In the few firsthand printed reports of the epidemics known to exist, colonists described scenes of utter chaos and desolation: bodies lying in streets and in houses because no one had buried them and a handful of survivors from previously bustling villages.[79]

Some Natives seem to have connected the epidemics with the colonists' arrival: Tisquantum informed the Wampanoags that the colonists kept disease in their storehouse for gunpowder and sent it out whenever they wished. In 1648, English missionaries recorded a Native man's account of his dream concerning the "great mortality" that preceded the colonists' arrival.[80] In his dream:

'he did think he saw a great many men come to those parts in cloths, just as the *English* now are appareled, and among them there arose up a man all in black, with a thing in his hand which he now sees was all one *English* mans

77. Salisbury, *Manitou and Providence,* 102–3.
78. See Crosby, "Virgin Soil Epidemics," 290.
79. Although colonists described the epidemics only as the "plague," it is unlikely that the bubonic plague could have survived an Atlantic crossing. Other possibilities include chickenpox, viral hepatitis, or a combination of diseases. For such references, see *Good News,* 10 and 18, and the selections from Dermer and Morton in section 3. For contemporary studies, see Hoornbeek, "Investigation into the Cause or Causes"; Cook, "Significance of Disease"; and Robinson, et al., "Preliminary Biocultural Interpretations." For debates about the contact-era illnesses as "virgin soil" epidemics, or those that spread quickly because Natives lacked immunity to them, see Crosby, "Virgin Soil Epidemics"; Jones, *Rationalizing Epidemics;* and Kelton, *Epidemics and Enslavement.*
80. Shepard, *Clear Sun-shine,* 10.

book; this black man he said stood upon a higher place than all the rest, and on the one side of him were the *English*, on the other a great number of *Indians*: this man told all the *Indians* that God was *moosquantum* or angry with them, and that he would kill them for their sins.'[81]

The connection that the dream drew between the epidemics and divine anger seems to have been shared by many Native peoples, for whom the epidemics appeared to be a sign of divine judgment for inappropriate behavior.[82] In particular, they seem to have interpreted the diseases as a sign of the displeasure of one of their deities, known as Kiehtan (or, as the Narragansetts called him, Cautantowwit). Kiehtan was associated with the southwest and with corn and harvests; he also sometimes cured disease. Winslow reported that when the Wampanoags desired to "obtain any great matter, [they would] meet together, and cry unto him [Kiehtan], and so likewise for plenty . . . and hang up Garlands and other things in memory of the same."[83] During the epidemics, many Natives found that Kiehtan did not heed their requests for healing, notwithstanding powahs' reliance on fasting and dreaming to seek out new rituals that would counter the illnesses. Wampanoag and Massachusett peoples, in particular, concluded that Kiehtan was "angry and sends [diseases], whom none can cure" on them while preserving other nations, particularly the Narragansett.[84] As a result, they "grow more and more cold in their worship to *Kiehtan*; saying in their memory he was much more called upon" than he was after the epidemics.[85] To acknowledge the deity's favor to them, the Narragansetts honored Cautantowwit by creating a "great spacious house wherein only some few (that are as we may term them Priests) come" and offering sacrifices.[86]

The epidemics created a crisis of authority for both powahs and sachems. Both leaders obtained their status through reciprocal relations. People gave gifts to powahs in order to obligate them to call on non-human spirits and to cure their diseases; they paid tribute to sachems in

---

81. Ibid.
82. On this dream, see also Brown, *Pilgrim and the Bee*, 206–7.
83. Winslow, *Good News*, 53.
84. Ibid.
85. Ibid., 55.
86. Ibid.

exchange for leadership and the distribution of resources to those in need. When powahs proved unable to cure disease or themselves fell prey to illness, as they did during the epidemics, they could lose their authority as medical practitioners.[87] Moreover, the epidemics changed the formerly strong position that the Massachusetts and the Wampanoags had enjoyed by weakening them demographically and politically. Massasoit and ten of his pnieses submitted to the Narragansetts, who assumed a new position of strength and influence in Narragansett Bay. The Wampanoags acknowledged this power by giving up their position at the head, or northern side, of Narragansett Bay and by paying tribute to Canonacus, the Narragansett sachem. By 1620, Massasoit's lands were on the eastern side of Narragansett Bay, while the Massachusetts' village was to the north, near what is today called Massachusetts Bay; the Narragansetts held (and many Narragansett people still live on) the western side of Narragansett Bay.[88] (Figure 2)

Like the Wampanoags, the colonists were both physically and politically weak by 1621. Illness and famine during their first winter in New England had reduced their original group of 102 colonists to half that number; ongoing food shortages made starvation a threat to the survivors.[89] And, like the Natives who lived through the epidemics of 1616–1619, the colonists drew connections between their physical maladies and their spiritual health. Illness signified divine judgment or displeasure, and spiritual maladies, or sin, had to be purged before physical maladies would be fully healed. Yet the similar views that Natives and colonists held of the supernatural origins of illness did not always extend to the environment and its role in disease and healing. Native peoples viewed the environment as a natural and spiritual resource with which they could construct and maintain the relationships that were necessary for physical and spiritual health, but colonists held that the New World's natural environment posed a potential hazard to their health and English

87. See Starna, "Biological Encounter," 514–15.
88. On post-epidemic shifts in power and relations between the Narragansetts and Wampanoags, including Massasoit's submission to the Narragansetts, see Salisbury, *Manitou and Providence*, 105–6.
89. The group of colonists was composed of thirty Separatists and seventy-two "strangers," colonists who had traveled to New England with financial profit as their primary goal.

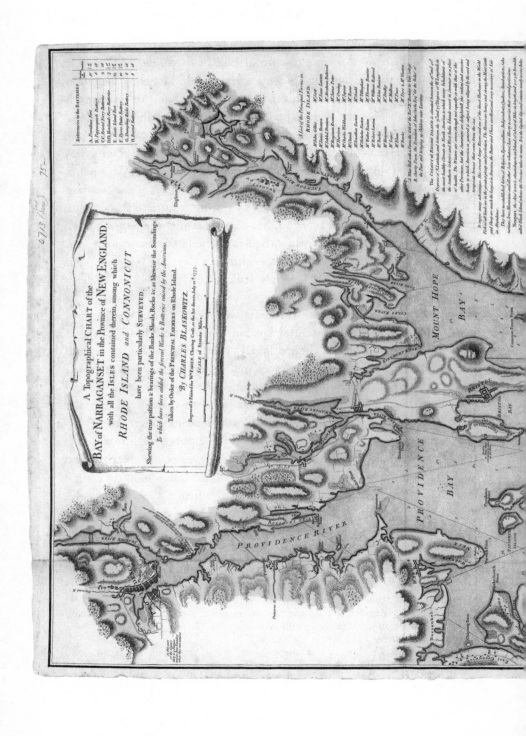

References to the Batteries

A. *Providence Fort*
B. *Pepperganset Battery*
CC. *Bristol Ferry Batteries*
DD. *Howland Ferry Batteries*
E. *Gould Island Battery*
F. *Dyers Point Battery*
G. *Dumpling Rocks Battery*
H. *Bristol Battery*

A List of the Principal Farms in
RHODE ISLAND.

Mr *John Collins*
Mr *Lewis Preston*
Mr *Lebdiel Brenton*
Mr *Benjamin Brenton*
Mr *Harrison*
Mr *Charles Wickham*
Mr *Powell*
Mr *Honeyman Easton*
Mr *Nicholas Easton*
Mr *Walter Easton*
Mr *Rodale*
Mr *Hammon*
Mr *Lopez*
Mr *Eliot*
Mr *Brenton*

Mr *Coate*
Mr *Isaac Lawton*
Mr *Abraham Redwood*
Mr *Vernon*
Mr *Overing*
Mr *Coleman*
Mr *Row*
Mr *Rome*
Mr *Whitehorse*
Mr *Thurston Brenton*
Mr *Robert Lawton*
Mr *John Brenton*
Mr *John Bannister*
Mr *Dudley*
Mr *Malbone*
Mr *Coggeshall*
Mr *Dyer & Mr Watson*

A Topographical CHART of the
BAY of NARRAGANSET in the Province of NEW ENGLAND.
with all the ISLES contained therein, among which
RHODE ISLAND and CONNONICUT
have been particularly SURVEYED.

Shewing the true position & bearings of the Banks Shoals Rocks &c. as likewise the Soundings:
To which have been added the several Works & Batteries raised by the Americans.
Taken by Order of the PRINCIPAL FARMERS on Rhode Island.

By CHARLES BLASKOWITZ.

Engraved & Printed for Wm FADEN, Charing Cross, as the Act directs, July 22d 1777.

Scale of Statute Miles.

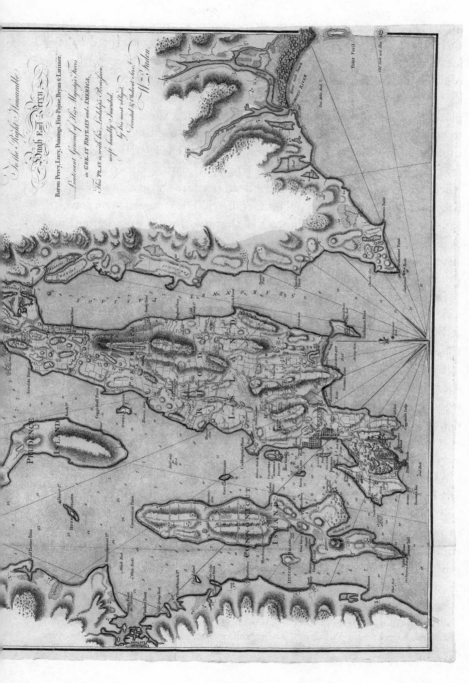

Figure 2. Charles Blaskowitz, *Plan de la baie de Narragansett dans la Nouvelle Angleterre* (1780). Courtesy of the John Carter Brown Library at Brown University.

identities. According to early modern European medical philosophies, the climate in which one was born shaped physical, mental, and behavioral characteristics, meaning that the environment was the foundation of national and personal traits. Travel to unfamiliar climates threatened to disrupt the balance of humors (or bodily fluids) determined by one's place of origin, with consequences that included sickness, physical alteration (such as changes in one's skin color or strength), and different— usually degenerate—behavior. These anxieties were particularly acute for colonists who traveled to hot or tropical climates that characterized places such as Virginia or the Caribbean because those climates starkly contrasted with England's cool temperatures. The colonists who traveled to New England were also concerned that the climate would alter their bodies, minds, and behavior, for Europeans believed that climate was consistent along lines of latitude, and New England's location aligned it with southern Europe rather than with England.[90]

The connection between environment and health was particularly significant for the Plimoth colonists, who held that their physical bodies had to be ordered or ruled in order to correct their souls' inherently sinful status. This conviction rested on a Calvinist view of soul and body as intimately connected: the body's actions reflected the state of the soul, for the body was driven by the desires of the heart. For the Separatists, salvation was not invisible to the human eye, as most Puritans argued, but was demonstrated in actions. Dissenters such as the Separatists concluded that a "true saint must remove his or her body, whose unstable humors were susceptible to its surroundings, from the corrupt body of the Anglican Church, for sin was transmitted *physically*, by participating in unholy worship."[91] After leaving the Church of England and facing punishment and imprisonment in England, they traveled to Amsterdam in 1608 and to Leiden in 1609, in an attempt to remove to a place distant from corruption, where they could create an environment suited to ordering and purifying both body and soul. However, the Separatists soon feared that their children were attracted to Dutch culture, and they decided to travel

---

90. On colonists' fears of the New World's climate, see Kupperman, "Fear of Hot Climates"; Kupperman, "Puzzle of the American Climate"; Chaplin, "Natural Philosophy and an Early Racial Idiom"; and Egan, *Authorizing Experience*, esp. chap. 1.

91. Finch, *Dissenting Bodies*, 143.

yet again, this time to the New World, where they hoped to be able to live free from the world's corruptions.

As they discovered, however, the threat of physical and moral degeneration traveled with them to New England. William Bradford explained in *Of Plymouth Plantation* that colonists worried that "change of air, diet, and drinking of water would infect their bodies with sore sicknesses, and grievous diseases."[92] Indeed, the New World's climate left its mark on the colonists' bodies. As they wrote in 1622: "cold and wet lodging had so tainted our people, for scarce any of us were free from vehement coughs, as if they should continue long in that estate, it would endanger the lives of many, and breed diseases and infection amongst us."[93] Moreover, their bodies rejected New England's food: "We found great Mussels, and very fat and full of Seapearl, but we could not eat them, for they made us all sick that did eat, as well sailors as passengers; they caused to cast and scour, but they were soon well again."[94]

Adding to the threat of bodily illness was the possibility that the physical strains of travel and the unfamiliar climate would manifest themselves in altered behavior. Robert Cushman, one of the colonists' deacons, or religious leaders, articulated concerns about moral degeneration in New England in a sermon delivered at Plimoth in 1621. He published his *Sermon Preached at Plimmoth Plantation in New England* on his return to England in 1622, making it one of the first printed accounts from the new colony. Cushman warned the colonists against the dangers of "self-love," or the practice of putting one's own welfare first.[95] Although he carefully stated that it was not his intent to "speak any thing, either in praise, or dispraise of the country," he predicted that colonists who were willing to work hard and who desired to convert the "Heathens" would prosper.[96] However, Cushman also warned that settlement in the New World could bring about undesirable changes in colonists' behavior, and he cited the

92. Bradford, *Of Plymouth Plantation,* 26.
93. *Relation or Journal,* 14.
94. Ibid., 2. In 1623, Emmanuel Altham, one of the investors in Plimoth colony, wrote that some travelers to New England "have had agues at the first coming over, but not sick above a week—and myself was ill for three or four days, but I thank these good friends of mine at the plantation, I am recovered pretty well, thanks be to God." See Altham, Emmanuel Altham to Sir Edward Altham, 28.
95. Cushman, *Sermon Preached at Plimoth,* 1.
96. Ibid., A2v.

example of settlers in Virginia as proof. As he explained, "It is reported, that there are many men gone to that other Plantation in *Virginia*, which, whilst they lived in England, seemed very religious, zealous, and conscionable; and have now lost even the sap of grace, and edge to all goodness; and are become mere worldlings."[97] Cushman warned the Plimoth colonists to monitor their behavior and their attitude toward others' needs in order to ensure that they did not degenerate.

Winslow certainly had Cushman's sermon and warnings about the effects of transatlantic travel in mind when writing *Good News*. Yet the task of convincing his readers that the colonists had not degenerated was made extremely difficult by the fact that the events of 1621–1623 contradicted earlier predictions and promotions and instead supported fears of the effects of travel to the New World. Stories of starvation and cross-cultural violence hardly lived up to earlier reports of plentiful resources and of peaceful relations with southern New England Natives.[98] Furthermore, the colonists' violent actions against the Massachusetts contradicted their claims to have founded a "healthful and hopeful" colony, one characterized not only by healthy people but also by "healthy," or virtuous, behavior.[99]

Winslow probably also responded to direct criticism of the colonists' actions from the Separatists' minister, John Robinson, who criticized the colonists in a letter to Bradford. The governor had informed Robinson of the attack by explaining that the Massachusetts' "wickedness came upon their own pate [or head]; we killed seven of the chief of them, and the head of one of them stands still on our fort for a terror unto others."[100] Far from responding with approval, however, Robinson critiqued these actions in a 1624 letter in which he called the colonists at Wessagusset "heathenish Christians" and lamented that the Plimoth colonists "had

---

97. Ibid., 11.

98. The colonists, including Winslow, made these predictions in the *Relation or Journal*, 60–64. See section 3. In addition, several travelers who stopped at Plimoth emphasized the ease with which fish and game could be obtained. See Pory, John Pory to the Earl of Southampton, 5–13; Pory, John Pory to the Governor of Virginia, 14–18; and Altham, Emmanuel Altham to Sir Edward Altham, 23–25.

99. Winslow, *Good News*, A2r.

100. William Bradford to John Robinson, in Burgess, *John Robinson*, 279. Winslow must have taken this letter to Robinson, for he traveled to England two days after Bradford dated the letter.

[not] converted some [Natives], before you had killed any."[101] Robinson further pointed out that "where blood is once begun to be shed; it is sel-dome stanched of a long time after," and he suggested that the colonists had taken the easier track of producing "terror to poor barbarous people" rather than that of winning them to Christianity and peace.[102] Even if Winslow did not read Robinson's response before sending *Good News* to press, he carried Bradford's letter to Europe and certainly corresponded with Robinson on his return to England. He must have known of the minister's disapproval when writing *Good News*.[103]

Meanwhile, the sixty colonists at Wessagusset, mostly indentured servants who had been sent to New England by Thomas Weston, one of the Plimoth colonists' associates, supported suspicions that the New World had undesirable effects on English bodies and behavior. Lacking sufficient provisions from the start due to Weston's financial difficulties, the Wessagusset men borrowed corn from Plimoth when they arrived, and they later bought and then stole corn from the Massachusetts. Some men had even gone so far as to leave the colony in order to live with and work for the Massachusetts in exchange for food. The Wessagusset colo-nists' food shortage was so acute, Winslow noted, that the Massachusetts had "filled our ears with clamours against them, for stealing their corn, and other abuses conceived by them," and the Plimoth colonists contin-ued to share some of their own meager food supplies with the hungry men.[104] But they did not offer this food willingly: they complained that the Wessagusset men refused to work, and Winslow described them as a *"disorderly Colony that are dispersed, and most of them returned, to the great prejudice and damage of him that set them forth; who as they were a stain to* old England *that bred them, in respect of their lives and manners amongst the* Indians."[105] Ultimately, Winslow lamented, "we knew no means to redress those abuses, save reproof, and advising them to better walking as occasion served."[106]

---

101. John Robinson to William Bradford, in Bradford, *Of Plymouth Plantation*, 375.
102. Ibid.
103. It is possible that Robinson received news of the attack directly from Winslow after hearing informal reports. Robinson stated in his letter to Bradford that he heard of the attack "at first by report, and since by more certain relation." See ibid.
104. Winslow, *Good News*, 14.
105. Ibid., A4r.
106. Ibid., 15.

Even as the Plimoth colonists claimed that they could not control the Wessagusset men's behavior, Winslow attempted to determine how their responses to that behavior and its consequences were received in England. In *Good News*, he offered evidence that the Plimoth settlers had not degenerated as, he suggested, the Wessagusset men had, and he worked to show that the colonists had deliberated carefully before deciding to attack the Massachusetts, that is, that their violence was not the result of quick passions or irrational decisions. Massasoit's tip about the Massachusetts' plan was crucial to Winslow's story, for Winslow offered the sachem's statement as evidence that the colonists had not acted without knowledge that they were in danger.

Compromise and Conflict

Although Winslow and Bradford argued that the Massachusetts brought the attack on themselves, violence was not inevitable in 1623. Indeed, for several years the colonists and Wampanoags had worked to establish mutually beneficial ways of interacting. These methods were certainly not devoid of conflict, but both peoples recognized the value of forming an alliance and maintaining peace in the region, even though both were also hesitant to make contact in 1620–21. The Wampanoags seem to have observed the colonists for some time before the settlers realized that their presence had not gone unnoticed. Colonial reconnaissance parties happened on small groups of Native men as they searched for food, wood, and a site for their settlement, and they noted fields that had been planted with corn, houses containing Native and European implements, traps, paths, and graves. Perhaps suspicious of travelers' usual practice of establishing trading relations and then kidnapping Wampanoag men, the Wampanoags watched the colonists from a distance, noting their difficulty finding a suitable place for settlement, their shortage of food supplies and consumption of Native stores of corn, and the burials of the many colonists who did not survive their first winter. Yet aside from a brief confrontation in the winter of 1620, both colonists and Natives avoided contact.

By September 1621, the Wampanoags seem to have decided that an alliance with the newcomers was desirable, perhaps because their own reduced numbers made them vulnerable to the Narragansetts, who then seemed a more threatening rival than the colonists.[107] Massasoit's pow-ahs conducted preliminary ceremonies, which may have been designed to determine whether an overture to the English would be successful, or to purge the Wampanoags of hostile feelings toward the colonists, or to drive the colonists away. Then Massasoit sent several emissaries to Patuxet. The colonists first noticed two men who "presented them selves upon the top of a hill, over against our Plantation, about a quarter of a mile and less, and made signs unto us to come to them."[108] They reacted by arming themselves and increasing their meager fortifications. Next, an Abenaki man named Samoset, who had already been trading with the English in what is now Maine, astonished the colonists by walking into the village "where we intercepted him not suffering him to go in, as undoubtedly he would, out of his boldness, he saluted us in English."[109] Samoset accepted English food and hospitality (and, in some cases, in-sisted on it when the colonists were reluctant to let him spend the night at Patuxet), and he soon returned with Tisquantum, who informed the colo-nists that Massasoit wished to meet with them. Both the colonists and the Wampanoags refused to send their respective leaders out to meet the other group, so Winslow went "to parley" with the Wampanoags instead, taking with him the governor's message that he desired peace and trade as well as gifts for Massasoit and his brother.[110] Massasoit accepted the gifts, and he subsequently formed an alliance with the colonists, in which both parties promised to act in peace toward and to protect one another, to re-store any stolen tools or other goods to their rightful owners, and to leave weapons behind when entering one another's villages.[111] For the Wampa-noags, allying with the English allowed them to resist the Narragansetts'

107. Neal Salisbury suggests that Massasoit traded corn and furs to Plimoth for the colony's protection from the Wampanoags' enemies and from the colony itself. Massasoit's overture thus seems to have been intended not only to protect his people from the Narragansetts but also to ensure that Plimoth would behave as his ally. See Salisbury, *Manitou and Providence*, 117, as well as Donohue, *Bradford's Indian Book*, 15.

108. *Relation or Journal*, 31.

109. Ibid., 32.

110. Ibid., 36.

111. See the copies of the colonists' transcriptions of this alliance in section 1; as the texts show, different colonists represented its terms in different ways.

demands and to recover some of their power in the area, although they soon discovered that the English could be demanding allies.

From the colonists' perspective, the treaty provided them with respected allies, especially important given their ignorance of local politics and difficulty finding food. However, the colonists seem to have misunderstood or only partially understood both the nature of Massasoit's influence in the region and the significance of the alliance for the Wampanoags. The writers of *Mourt's Relation* referred to Massasoit as a king, a title that suggested that he had authority over particular land and people but that did not accurately reflect the sachem's combination of responsibility and power. Massasoit's authority depended on his personality and leadership and on his ability to maintain the respect of lower sachems and military leaders. He led the Pokanoket Wampanoags from his village at Sowams, and area Wampanoag sachems had pledged their alliance in exchange for his protection and direction. Massasoit had great power within these villages, but he was also responsible for providing resources and for preserving peace. His prestige thus lay more in his ability to maintain relationships through tribute and gifts than in his control of a particular area of land or acts of conquest. Massasoit's sachemship was certainly associated with particular locations, but these areas were identified less by specific boundaries than by "various resource-locations and topographic features."[112]

Moreover, some of the colonists' written records reflect their sense that, by entering into the treaty, Massasoit "subscribed obedience to our Sovereign Lord King JAMES."[113] By contrast, Massasoit probably viewed the treaty as an agreement that cemented bonds of reciprocity in addition to defining the colonists and Wampanoags as allies. Indeed, the colonists were surprised when Wampanoag people began traveling frequently to Plimoth, with the expectation that the colonists would provide them with food and lodging. For the Wampanoags, these exchanges were means of confirming and strengthening their relationship with the colonists. Winslow eventually requested that Massasoit restrain his people from

---

112. Bragdon and Goddard, *Native Writings*, 3–4. On Native and colonial views of this treaty and the relationship between Natives, colonists, and, by extension, King James, see Pulsipher, "'Subjects . . . Unto the Same King.'"

113. Cushman, *Sermon Preached at Plimoth*, A3v.

their frequent visits, but the colonists also recognized that participating in such exchanges was necessary to their survival.

In addition to misunderstanding the meaning of Massasoit's power, the colonists may also have misinterpreted the Massachusetts' actions and Native discussions of violence. The colonists were far from adept at understanding Native actions and intentions, for as Winslow admitted, they often failed to distinguish between rumors and accurate news, and they were quick to credit accounts of Native hostility that turned out to be false. For example, Winslow reported that in 1621–22, the colonists feared on multiple occasions that various groups of Natives had joined in a conspiracy against them, much as they later feared that the Massachusetts had joined with nearby tribes and were planning to attack Wessagusset and Plimoth. In some cases, such as when the Narragansetts sent a bundle of arrows wrapped in snakeskin to Plimoth, the colonists argued that they had reason to be concerned; in others, they discovered that they had credited rumors. In the case of the arrows, Tisquantum advised the colonists that they signaled hostile intentions, and the colonists filled the bundle with gunpowder and shot and returned it.[114] However, the Narragansett sachem Canonacus refused to accept the bundle, and it traveled throughout the region until it was returned to the colonists. By refusing to accept the bundle, the Narragansetts also refused the colonists' challenge. The Narragansetts were certainly not the colonists' allies (in fact, Plimoth probably alienated them by forming an alliance with their rivals, the Wampanoags), but they did seem to put hostilities aside for the time being by refusing to accept the bundle.[115] Furthermore, as Tisquantum's ability to convince the colonists that Massasoit was preparing to attack them shows, Plimoth colonists responded to rumors of

---

114. It is possible that Tisquantum misinterpreted the meaning of the arrows, whether purposely or not. The Iroquois Constitution defines five bound arrows as a symbol of unity and strength: "Five arrows shall be bound together very strong and each arrow shall represent one nation. As the five arrows are strongly bound this shall symbolize the complete union of the nations. Thus are the Five Nations united completely and enfolded together, united into one head, one body, and one mind. Therefore they shall labor, legislate and council together for the interest of future generations." Algonquian and Iroquois people had different political and cultural practices, but the Iroquois symbol raises the possibility that alternate interpretations of the arrows also existed in New England. See Parker, *Constitution of the Five Nations*, 45.

115. See Salisbury, *Manitou and Providence*, 122–23.

violence and deception by assuming that they were true. In response to Tisquantum's account of Massasoit's league with the Narragansetts, the colonists quickly returned to their village, where they made three guns ready and fortified the village against what they thought was an impending attack. Later, when news came from Massasoit and from Phenehas Pratt, one of the Wessagusset colonists, of an impending attack from the Massachusetts, the colonists reacted in much the same way, by preparing for and, in this case, executing, violence without receiving confirmation from the Massachusetts that the reports were true.

Colonists' tendency to assume that Natives intended to attack them was particularly problematic because Natives sometimes used rumors to bring about desired ends without resorting to bloodshed. As English colonist Thomas Morton explained in 1637, the Massachusett sachem Chickataubut (also known as Obtakiest after 1623) used rumors to protect his interests and to secure his sovereignty over trading networks. Annoyed that Narragansett men were trading on his land but not strong enough to confront them directly, Chickataubut circulated rumors among the English colonists living nearby that the Narragansetts' true intent was to examine the colonists' strength and to watch for an opportunity to attack them. He requested that the English wear their armor for protection and then brought a Narragansett trader to see the colonists, who appeared to be prepared for war. The Narragansetts, fearing what seemed to be an imminent attack from the English, left the trading networks to the Massachusetts.[116]

Alternatively, Natives used rumors as practical jokes and messages about the ways that information circulated in New England. For example, after one of Winslow's visits to Sowams, Massasoit sent word to Plimoth that Winslow had died on his journey home. The colonists were thus surprised when Winslow arrived at Plimoth a few days later. When asked about his message, Massasoit responded that "it was their [Natives'] manner to do so, that they might be more welcome when they came home."[117] As Matt Cohen has pointed out, Massasoit's misinformation highlighted the colonists' reliance on Winslow while also "remind[ing] the English that though they have escaped death, they have not yet mastered local

116. See Morton, *New English Canaan*, 44–45.
117. Winthrop, *Journal of John Winthrop*, 125.

information systems and that a Native audience is aware that its 'maner' is being observed."[118]

Given Natives' practice of using rumors to accomplish ends in non-violent or even humorous ways, it is possible that the Massachusetts' threats against the Wessagusset colonists were intended to frighten them or to make them respect the sovereignty of Massachusett food supplies. What the colonists often interpreted as subtlety or treacherousness thus might have actually been strategies for preserving sovereignty through nonviolent means. Indeed, when the Plimoth men arrived at Wessagusset to attack the Massachusetts, they found several colonists who were living with the Massachusetts, apparently without any concern for their safety. When questioned "how they durst so leave the ship and live in such security," the Wessagusset men "answered like men senseless of their own misery, they feared not the *Indians*, but lived and suffered them to lodge with them, not having sword, or gun, or needing the same."[119] What Winslow and other colonists interpreted as senselessness may indeed have been desperation, but it seemed to derive more from lack of food than from fear of the Massachusetts.

But it is also possible that the Massachusetts were indeed planning to attack Wessagusset and Plimoth. Massasoit and Winslow must have known that the Massachusetts' anger at the colonists in both locations was justified. The Wessagusset men had confessed to taking food from the Massachusetts, and the colony's leaders admitted that they could not keep their men from continuing to steal. Furthermore, the Wessagusset men failed to follow local systems of justice when punishing the thieves: they offered to hand over the offender to the Massachusett sachem, but he protested that the Wessagusset men should first punish the offender themselves. As Pratt wrote, the sachem explained: "yt [it] is not just dealing. If my men wrong my neighbor sachem or his men he sends me word & I beat or kill my men according to the offence. If his men wrong me or my men I send him word & he beats or kills his men According to the offence. All Sachems do Justice by their own men. If not we say they are all Agreed & then we fight, & now I say you all steal my Corn."[120] The

---

118. Cohen, *Networked Wilderness*, 88.

119. Winslow, *Good News*, 41.

120. Pratt, *Declaration of the Affairs*.

Wessagusset men had failed to do "justice by their own men" when they avoided responsibility for punishing the thieves. For the Massachusetts, if a sachem failed to punish his own men according to the offense, he could agree that a fight between the groups was an appropriate means of resolving the conflict. Thus, although Winslow presented the Massachusetts' threats as excessive, from a Native perspective the sachem had followed local practices of justice by bringing complaints against the colonists, only to see the colonists fail to punish the offenders.

The Massachusetts also knew that the colonists had already contemplated an attack on them. In February 1622, John Sanders, the leader of the Wessagusset colonists, sent a letter to Bradford in which he explained that he had little food and complained that the Massachusetts had refused to loan corn to them. Sanders proposed that the colonists attack the Massachusetts together, in order to save his men from famine and to establish their authority over area food supplies. But Bradford, hearing from the Massachusett messenger who brought Sanders's message that the Natives had only enough corn for the winter and spring planting, advised against violence at that time. News of Sanders's plan made their way to the Massachusetts, who grew increasingly concerned about both Plimoth's and Wessagusset's intentions.[121]

Disagreements about food aside, the Massachusetts had good reason to be angry with the Plimoth colonists, who had dishonored several Massachusett graves shortly after their arrival in New England. Thomas Morton wrote that the colonists had offended Chickataubut by disturbing his mother's grave while they were searching for stores of corn during the winter of 1620–21. Morton explained that the colonists had "defaced the monument of the dead at Pasonayessit (by taking away the hearse Cloth which was two great Bears skins sewed together at full length, and propped up over the grave of Chuatawbacks [Chickataubut's] mother)."[122] Morton noted that Chickataubut called his men together and told them of a dream he had in which his mother appeared to him and asked if they could "forget to take revenge of those wild people, that hath my monu-

---

121. See Winslow, *Good News*, 34–37, and Bradford, *Of Plymouth Plantation*, 114–15. According to Bradford, some of the Wessagusset men informed the Massachusetts that the colonists considered taking food by force. See also Salisbury, *Manitou and Providence*, 127–29.

122. Morton, *New English Canaan*, 106.

ment defaced in despiteful manner, disdaining our ancient antiquities, and honourable Customs."[123]

Morton's disdain for the Plimoth colonists may have influenced his account of Chickataubut's anger, but the colonists themselves admitted that they had disturbed several graves. As the writers of *Mourt's Relation* explained, the colonists had stumbled on the graves while looking for corn. They described in detail two graves, one of which held many funeral objects, from a bow to iron objects, a knife, and a needle, as well as the bones and skull of a man with yellow hair; another grave held the bones of a child.[124] As the colonists noted, the bodies were sewn into mats, a common burial practice in southern New England.[125] The bodies in these graves were probably buried facing the southwest—the direction toward which the souls of the dead traveled—and in a flexed position, to signify the parallels between birth and death as moments of movement into and out of the natural world. The colonists explained that after finding the two graves, they: "digged in sundry like places, but found no more Corn, nor any things else but graves."[126] Later in their explorations, the colonists stumbled across a "great burying place" that was "full of Graves, some bigger, and some less."[127] It is possible that one of these graves belonged to Chickataubut's mother or other Massachusett people and that the Massachusetts would have had reasons beyond circumventing a counterattack for taking action against Plimoth after they attacked Wessagusset.

After 1623: Ongoing Encounters

With the attack on the Massachusetts, the Plimoth colonists positioned themselves as a significant power in New England. If their actions fostered

123. Ibid., 107. Erik R. Seeman suggests that the colonists' removal of the bearskin marker for Chickataubut's mother's grave was considered an act of defacement and desecration. As he suggests, the colonists may have been acting on their belief that burial rituals should be simple (unlike Catholic ceremonies). See Seeman, *Death in the New World*, 151–53.

124. Seeman suggests that this grave held the remains of a Frenchman who lived as a captive among the Massachusetts before the Plimoth colonists arrived. See Seeman, *Death in the New World*, 145–48. And, see Pratt's account of this French captive in section 1.

125. See Simmons, *Cautantowwit's House*, chap. 4, especially 58–61.

126. *Relation or Journal*, 11.

127. Ibid., 17.

resentment against the English, it also impressed the Natives with the colonists' willingness to use violence to obtain their goals. As Winslow noted, some New England Natives were so shocked by the colonists' actions that they left their homes and lived in swamps or deserted locations. Moreover, Massasoit's decision to relate information about the Massachusetts' plan established him as a trustworthy ally and cemented the Pokanoket Wampanoag–Plimoth relationship. The colony at Wessagusset "dissolved" when the surviving men either returned to England or, in a few cases, were incorporated into Plimoth colony.[128] However, in the years following *Good News*'s publication in 1624, the colonists at Plimoth did not always maintain their position of strength, especially with the arrival of colonists at Massachusetts Bay and with the Pequots' rising power and control over trading networks in the 1620s and early 1630s. The Plimoth colonists and the Wampanoags did maintain their alliance, although this relationship was frequently put to the test. It would finally disintegrate in 1675, when Massasoit's second son, Metacom, or Philip, led a pan-tribal force against the United Colonies (Massachusetts Bay, Plimoth, Connecticut, and New Haven) in what came to be called King Philip's War.

Winslow continued to play a leading role in Plimoth Colony's governance and in both colonial and English dealings with New England Natives. He worked to establish trading posts for Plimoth on the Connecticut River in the late 1620s, with the goal of trading with the Pequots. Winslow served as governor of Plimoth in 1633, 1636, and 1644; he frequently served as a magistrate, and he was appointed agent for the United Colonies. He traveled to England in 1646 in this capacity to present and defend the colonies' interests, just as he had when writing *Good News*. In some cases, his duties included defending himself from charges that he had overstepped his authority while colonial governor: in 1635, he was briefly imprisoned for performing marriages and teaching in the church at Plimoth, despite the fact that he was not a minister. Winslow continued to serve English imperial interests until his death: he traveled as a commissioner on an expedition aimed at taking Hispaniola from the Spanish. He fell ill and died during these travels, and he was buried at sea in 1655, off the coast of Jamaica.[129]

---

128. Winslow, *Good News*, 47.

129. On Winslow's career after the 1620s, see Bangs, *Pilgrim Edward Winslow*, chaps. 5, 7–11, and Field, *Errands into the Metropolis*, 61–70.

Although he did not return to New England after traveling to London in 1646, Winslow maintained his interest in cross-cultural relations and in Native American religious practices. In particular, he employed his observations of Natives' religious beliefs and collected others' accounts in order to solicit English support for missions to the Natives. In the late 1640s, Winslow published three tracts that collected writings by the colonial minister John Eliot and his associates. The ministers reported their progress converting New England Algonquians, especially Wampanoag and Massachusett peoples, with the goal of eliciting financial support for these projects from supporters in England.[130] In the preface to one of these tracts, *The Glorious Progress of the Gospel*, Winslow articulated his view that the Natives were members of the lost tribes of Israel, an opinion held by many English Puritans in both the New and the Old Worlds. He noted that he had observed that the Natives practiced certain ceremonies described in the "Law of Moses, about the purification of women, which no men at this day do observe, nor beside the Jews were ever known in that strictness to observe, as these Indians there daily do."[131] The conversion of Natives, and thus, some argued, of the Jews, would signal the imminent return of Christ and his thousand-year reign, an event many Puritans believed was also signaled by the death of Charles I, the English Civil Wars, and Cromwell's Interregnum government. The project to bring Natives to Christianity thus implicitly claimed that New England would play a key role in the millennium, or end times, for as Winslow and other colonists argued, establishing missions was key not only for Native souls but also for English Protestantism. He was instrumental in bringing a request for funding before Parliament, which led to the 1649 formation of the Society for the Propagation of the Gospel in New England. Funds from the Society financed several missions throughout New England, as well as the printing of John Eliot's translation of the Bible in Algonquian.[132] (Figure 3)

130. See Clark, introduction to *The Eliot Tracts*, 11–12.
131. Winslow, *Glorious Progress of the Gospel*, A3v–A4r.
132. See *Holy Bible*. On seventeenth-century missions to Natives in New England, see Bross, *Dry Bones and Indian Sermons*. Bross points out that as people in New and Old England began to question their justification for colonizing New England, missions to the Natives provided one way in which to argue for the validity and sustainability of the colonies. See also Silverman, *Faith and Boundaries*, and Rivett, *The Science of the Soul*, esp. chap. 3.

Figure 3. School of Robert Walker, *Edward Winslow*. Oil on Canvas. England, 1651. Pilgrim Hall Museum, Plymouth, Mass. PHM 0053, Gift of Abby Frothingham Gay Winslow, 1883.

New England Natives responded in different ways to English missions as well as to the colonists' expansion into area trading networks and onto their land. Some Native people chose to convert to Christianity and to live in "Praying Towns" with other converts. However, Massasoit seems to have refused to accept the colonists' religious practices. The missionaries

John Eliot and Thomas Mayhew made several references to a "great *Sachem* on the *Main*" (or mainland) who discouraged his people from converting.[133] Massasoit's decision to oppose Christianity suggests that, despite his alliance with Plimoth and his familiarity with English cultural practices, Native religious practices remained more relevant for him. Furthermore, Massasoit's success discouraging his people from converting to Christianity reflects his ongoing influence over his people and over colonial affairs.

Although the colonists dispossessed the Wampanoags and other Native peoples in New England through land deeds and warfare, Wampanoags continued to work to maintain sovereignty over their land, their history, and their language, sometimes by engaging with colonists and U.S. Americans, as Massasoit did, sometimes by engaging in violence, as Metacom (or Philip) did in 1675, and sometimes by employing Christianity to avoid cross-cultural violence, as the Wampanoags on Martha's Vineyard did during King Philip's War.[134] Furthermore, Massasoit's decision to aid the colonists and the Plimoth settlers' subsequent violence were invoked in the nineteenth century by Native writers and orators, who described the ongoing repercussions of colonial encounters. In his "Eulogy on King Philip," the Pequot and Methodist minister William Apess pointed out that, although Europeans had kidnapped Native men and boys, unjustly claimed a land that belonged to the Wampanoags, and denigrated Wampanoag people as inferior beings, Massasoit treated them with hospitality and kindness. As Apess commented, "Had it not been for this humane act of the Indians, every white man would have been swept from the New England colonies. In their sickness, too, the Indians were as tender to them as to their own children; and for all this, they were denounced as savages by those who had received all the acts of kindness they possibly could show them."[135] Finally, against colonists' and U.S. Americans' claims that the 1616–1619 epidemics and King Philip's War had entirely removed Natives from New England, the Wampanoags are an active, vibrant presence in New England, as indicated by projects such as the Wôpanâak (or Wampanoag) Language Reclamation Project,

133. Eliot, *Tears of Repentance*, C3r.
134. See Silverman, *Faith and Boundaries*, chap. 3.
135. Apess, "Eulogy on King Philip," 108.

organizations such as the Mashpee Wampanoag Indian Museum, and
events such as the yearly Mashpee Wampanoag Powwow.[136]

{oↄↄ}

The related texts that follow *Good News* illuminate Natives' and colonists'
various responses to new experiences as well as the challenges both peoples faced in the early decades of the seventeenth century. The first section
includes accounts of Native captives who were taken from New England
prior to the Plimoth colonists' arrival. The texts in section two detail the
illnesses that both New England Natives and the Plimoth colonists experienced, the Natives between 1616 and 1619 and the Plimoth colonists
in the early 1620s. This section likewise highlights the colonists' concerns
about moral illness, or degenerate behavior, anxieties that intensified after
the attack on the Massachusetts. Finally, section three details the first
contacts between the Wampanoags and the Plimoth colonists, contacts in
which both peoples were uncertain about the other party's intentions and
about how to proceed. Despite this uncertainty, both the colonists and
the Wampanoags established a relationship through official agreements
and shared hospitality. This section also includes Wessagusset colonist
Phenehas Pratt's account of the days leading up to the colonists' attack
and minister John Robinson's response to the colonists' violence.

Note on the Text

The John Carter Brown Library (shelf mark D 624 W 778g) copy of
the first (1624) edition of *Good News*, printed by John Dawson of Eliot's
Court Press, London, for John Bellamie and William Bladen, also of
London, served as copy text for this edition. Page 67 is misnumbered 59,
and a "Postscript" advertising two books sold by Bellamie follows the text
of *Good News*. A bifolium containing the second (1624) edition title page
and including the "brief relation of a credible intelligence of the present
estate of Virginia" promised on that new title page is bound with this
copy. For the second edition, the title page was reset to include the line

---

136. See the Mashpee Wampanoag website, http://mashpeewampanoagtribe.com,
and the site for the Wôpanâak Language Reclamation Project, http://wlrp.org.

"Whereunto is added by him a brief Relation of a credible intelligence of the present estate of *Virginia*" and the "Postscript" was cut. The JCBL copy was collated against a first edition held at the Boston Public Library, with which it was found to be typographically identical, and then against a copy of the second edition at the Massachusetts Historical Society.[137]

The text of the present edition reproduces the title page for the first edition and includes the advertisements in the "Postscript." The "brief Relation" appears after the "Postscript." Winslow's marginal note regarding Native religious practices appears as a footnote; a reproduction of the page from *Good News* that includes the marginal note appears nearby. The text has been lightly edited for consistency and clarity. Words have been silently modernized when these changes did not alter the meaning of the text. There are many variant spellings for words such as Plimoth, Puckanokick (or Pokanoket), Wessagusset (also Wesaguscus or Wichaguscusset), Hobbamock, Pecksuot, and pniese; these spellings have been regularized in accordance to the form most frequently used in the copy text. When the spelling did alter the meaning of the text (such as when Winslow referred to the "Massacheuseucks"), original spellings were retained. Capitalization and punctuation are reproduced from the copy text; a few spelling and punctuation errors or misprints have been silently corrected. Page numbers in brackets correspond to those in the copy text.

In the case of Phenehas Pratt's "Declaration," a photocopy of the manuscript held at the Massachusetts State Archives served as the copy text. The manuscript was collated against an 1858 transcription by Richard Frothingham Jr. held at the John Carter Brown Library. Because Pratt's inconsistent spellings and punctuation as well as the poor quality of the manuscript make it difficult to decipher some words, several gaps exist in the text. These gaps are signaled in this edition by ellipses, and missing words are supplied in brackets when they are suggested by context. Spellings have been modernized when doing so did not affect

---

137. Seven copies of the first edition and ten copies of the second edition exist in special collections. In addition to examining copies at the John Carter Brown Library, the Boston Public Library, and the Massachusetts Historical Society, I consulted librarians at the Huntington Library, the British Library, the Library Company of Philadelphia, the Newberry Library, and the New York Public Library.

the meaning of the text. Pratt used little punctuation in his "Declaration"; instead, he separated sentences with dashes or simply ran them together. Because Pratt's manuscript is already difficult to decipher, I have followed Frothingham by including periods where Pratt seems to have ended a sentence. However, I have retained Pratt's dashes, which separate thoughts or sentences.

Part I

EDWARD WINSLOW, *GOOD NEWS FROM NEW ENGLAND* (1624)

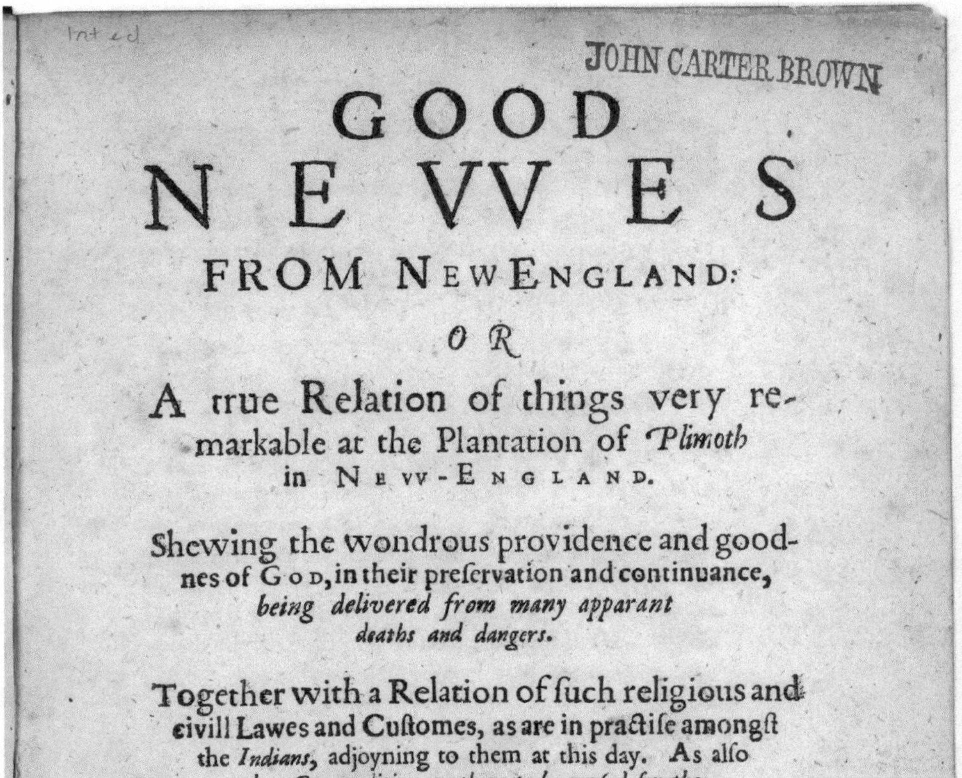

Int ed

JOHN CARTER BROWN

GOOD
NEVVES

FROM NEW ENGLAND:

OR

A true Relation of things very remarkable at the Plantation of *Plimoth*
in NEVV-ENGLAND.

Shewing the wondrous providence and good-
nes of GOD, in their prefervation and continuance,
*being delivered from many apparant
deaths and dangers.*

Together with a Relation of fuch religious and
civill Lawes and Cuftomes, as are in practife amongft
the *Indians*, adjoyning to them at this day. As alfo
*what Commodities are there to be rayfed for the
maintenance of that and other Plantations in the faid Country.*

Written by *E. W.* who hath borne a part in the
fore-named troubles, and there liued fince
their firft Arrivall.

LONDON

Printed by *I. D.* for *William Bladen* and *John Bellamie*, and
are to be fold at their Shops, at the *Bible* in *Pauls*-Church-
yard, and at the three Golden Lyons in Corn-hill,
neere the *Royall Exchange.* 1624.

Figure 4. Edward Winslow, *Good News*, title page, first edition (1624). Courtesy of the John
Carter Brown Library at Brown University.

GOOD
NEWS
FROM NEW ENGLAND:

OR

A true Relation of things very remarkable
at the Plantation of *Plimoth*
in NEW-ENGLAND.

Shewing the wondrous providence and goodness
of GOD, in their preservation and continuance,
*being delivered from many apparent
deaths and dangers.*

Together with a Relation of such religious and
civil Laws and Customs, as are in practise amongst
the *Indians*, adjoining to them at this day. As also
*what Commodities are there to be raised for the
maintenance of that and other Plantations
in the said Country.*

Written by *E.W.* who hath borne a part in the
fore-named troubles, and there lived since
their first Arrival.

LONDON

Printed by *J.D.* for *William Bladen* and *John Bellamie*, and
are to be sold at their Shops, at the *Bible* in *Pauls*-Church-yard,
and at the three Golden Lions in Corn-hill,
near the *Royall Exchange.* 1624. [Figures 4 and 5]

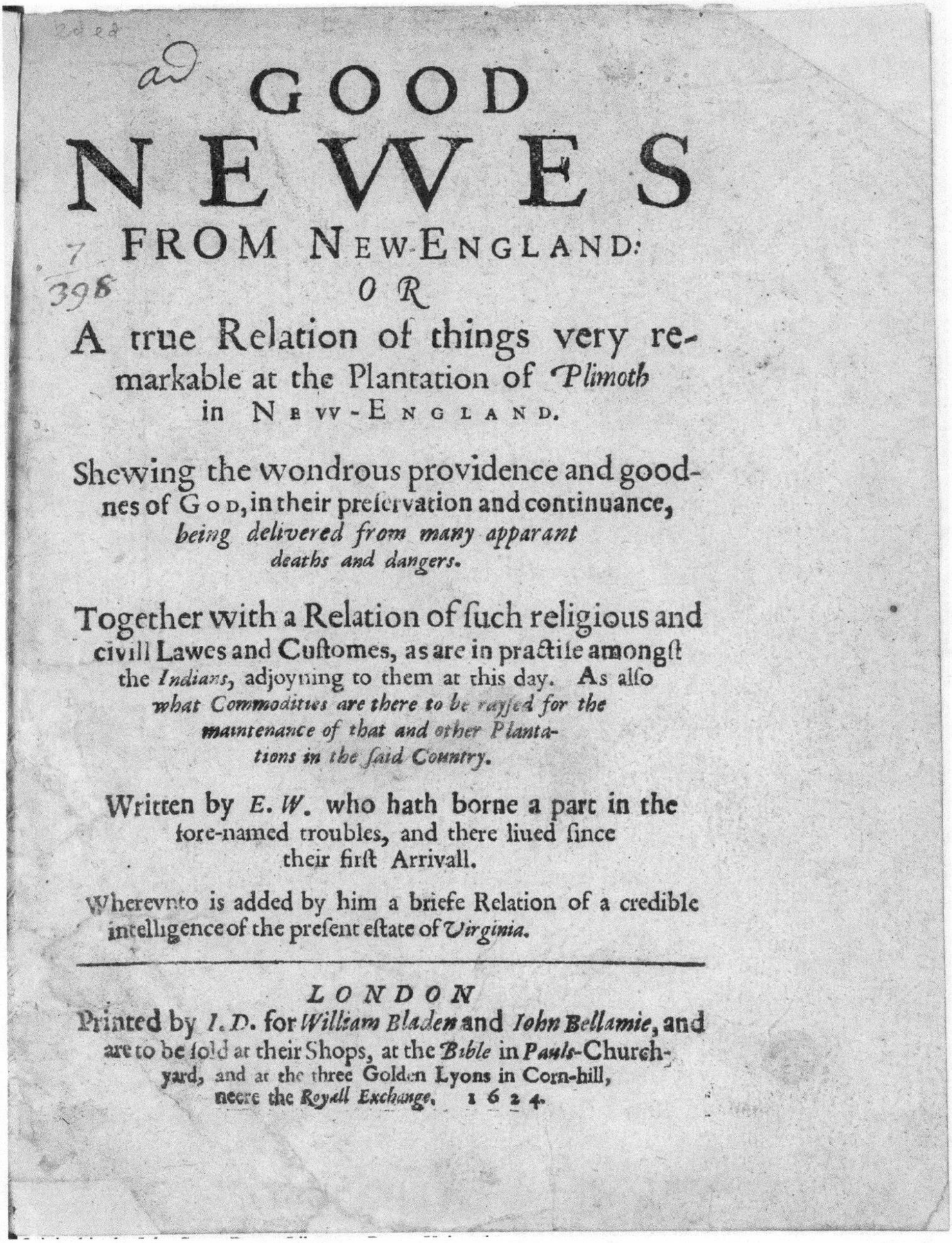

GOOD
NEWES

FROM New-England:

OR

A true Relation of things very remarkable at the Plantation of *Plimoth*
in New-England.

Shewing the wondrous providence and good-
nes of God, in their preservation and continuance,
being delivered from many apparant
deaths and dangers.

Together with a Relation of such religious and
civill Lawes and Customes, as are in practise amongst
the *Indians*, adjoyning to them at this day. As also
what Commodities are there to be rayted for the
maintenance of that and other Planta-
tions in the said Country.

Written by *E. W.* who hath borne a part in the
fore-named troubles, and there liued since
their first Arrivall.

Wherevnto is added by him a briefe Relation of a credible
intelligence of the present estate of *Virginia.*

LONDON

Printed by *I. D.* for *William Bladen* and *Iohn Bellamie*, and
are to be sold at their Shops, at the *Bible* in *Pauls*-Church-
yard, and at the three Golden Lyons in Corn-hill,
neere the *Royall Exchange.* 1624.

Figure 5. Edward Winslow, *Good News*, title page, second edition (1624). Courtesy of the John
Carter Brown Library at Brown University.

TO
ALL WELL-WILLERS
AND FURTHERERS OF
Plantations in *New England:* especially
to such as ever have or desire to assist, the
people of Plimoth *in their just
proceedings, Grace, and Peace, be
multiplied.*

Right Honourable and Worshipful Gentlemen, or whatsoever: Since it hath pleased God to stir you up to be instruments of his glory, in so honourable an enterprise as the enlarging of his Majesties Dominions, by planting his loyal subjects in so healthful and hopeful a Country as *New-England* is; where the Church of God being seated in sincerity, there is no less hope of convincing the Heathen of their evil ways, and converting them to the true knowledge and worship of the living God, and so consequently the salvation of their souls by the merits of Jesus Christ, than else-where though it be much talked on, & lightly [A2r] or lamely prosecuted. I therefore think it but my duty to offer the view of our proceedings to your worthy considerations, having to that end composed them together thus briefly as you see; wherein to your great encouragement, you may behold the good providence of God working with you in our preservation from so many dangerous plots and treacheries, as have been intended against us; as also in giving his blessing so powerfully upon the weak means we had, enabling us with health and ability beyond expectation, in our greatest scarcities, and possessing the hearts of the Savages with astonishment and fear of us, whereas if God had let them loose, they might easily have swallowed us up, scarce being an handful in comparison of those forces they might have gathered together against us, which now by Gods blessing will be more hard and difficult, in regard our number of men is increased, our town better fortified, and our store better victualed.

Blessed therefore be his name, that hath done so great things for us, &
hath wrought so great a change amongst us.

Accept I pray you my weak endeavours, pardon my unskillfulness, and
bear with my plainness in the things I have handled. Be not discouraged
by our former necessities, but rather encouraged with us, hoping that as
God hath wrought with us in our beginning of this worthy Work, undertaken in his name and fear; so he will by us accomplish the same to
his glory and our comfort, if we neglect not the means. I confess, it hath
not been much less chargeable[1] to some of you, than hard [A2v] and
difficult to us, that have endured the brunt of the battle, and yet small
profits returned; only by Gods mercy we are safely seated, housed, and
fortified, by which means a great step is made unto gain, and a more direct
course taken for the same, than if at first we had rashly and covetously
fallen upon it.

Indeed, three things are the overthrow and bane (as I may term it) of
Plantations.

1. The vain expectation of present profit, which too commonly taketh
a principal seat in the heart and affection;[2] though Gods glory, &c. is
preferred before it in the mouth with protestation.

2. Ambition in their Governours and Commanders, seeking only to
make themselves great, and slaves of all that are under them, to maintain
a transitory base honour in themselves, which God oft punisheth with
contempt.

3. The carelessness of those that send over supplies of men unto them,
not caring how they be qualified: so that oft times they are rather the
Image of men endued with bestial, yea, diabolical affections, than the
Image of God, endued with reason, understanding, and holiness. I praise
God I speak not these things experimentally, by way of complaint of our
own condition, but having great cause on the contrary part to be thankful
to God for his mercies towards us: but rather, if there be any too desirous of gain, to entreat them to moderate their affections, and consider
that no man expecteth fruit before the tree be grown; advising all men,
that as they tender their own well-fare, [A3r] so to make choice of such

---

1. Burdensome. Now obsolete. See *Oxford English Dictionary*, 1st ed., s.v. "Chargeable," adj., 4.
2. Feelings.

to manage and govern their affairs, as are approved not to be seekers of themselves, but the common good of all for whom they are employed; and beseeching such as have the care of transporting men for the supply and furnishing of Plantations, to be truly careful in sending such as may further and not hinder so good an action. There is no godly honest man, but will be helpful in his kind, and adorn his profession with an upright life and conversation, which Doctrine of manners ought first to be Preached by giving good example to the poor Savage Heathens amongst whom they live. On the contrary part, what great offense hath been given by many profane men, who being but seeming Christians, have made Christ and Christianity stink in the nostrils of the poor Infidels, and so laid a stumbling block before them: *but woe be to them by whom such offenses come.*

These things I offer to your Christian considerations, beseeching you to make a good construction of my simple meaning, and take in good part this ensuing Relation, dedicating my self and it evermore unto your service; beseeching God to crown our Christian and faithful endeavours with his blessings temporal and eternal.

Yours in this service, ever to be commanded:

E.W.

To the Reader.

Good Reader, when I first penned this discourse, I intended it chiefly for the satisfaction of my private friends,[3] *but since that time have been persuaded to publish the same: And the rather, because of a disorderly Colony that are dispersed, and most of them returned, to the great prejudice and damage of him that set them forth; who as they were a stain to old* England *that bred them, in respect of their lives and manners amongst the* Indians: *So it is to be feared, will be no less to* New-England *in their vile and clamorous reports, because she would not foster them in their desired idle courses. I would not be understood to think there were no well-deserving persons amongst them: for of mine own knowledge it was a grief to some that they were so yoked; whose*

---

3. Probably John Robinson and other Separatists in Leiden or in London and possibly investors in Plimoth colony.

deserts[4] *as they were then suitable to their honest protestations, so I desire still may be, in respect of their just and true Relations.*

Peradventure thou wilt rather marvel that I deal so plainly, than any way doubt of the truth of this my Relation, yea it may be tax me therewith, as seeming rather to discourage men, than any way to further so noble an action? If any honest mind be discouraged, I am sorry, sure I am, I have given no just cause; and am so far from being discouraged my self, as I purpose to return forthwith. And for other light and vain persons, if they stumble hereat I have my desire, accounting it better for them and us that they keep where they are, as being unfit and unable to perform so great a task.

Some faults have escaped because I could not attend on the Press, which I pray thee correct as thou findest, and I shall account it as a favour unto me.

Thine E. W.

[1]

GOOD NEWS FROM New-England.

The Good Ship called the *Fortune*, which in the Month of *Novemb.* 1621. (blessed be God) brought us a new supply of 35. persons, was not long departed our Coast, ere the Great People of *Nanohigganset*,[5] which are reported to be many thousands strong, began to breathe forth many threats against us, not withstanding their desired and obtained peace with us in the fore-going summer. Insomuch as the common talk of our neighbor *Indians*[6] on all sides was of the preparation they made to come against us. In reason a man would think they should have now more cause to fear us than before our supply came: but though none of them were present, yet [2] understanding by others that they neither brought Arms nor other provisions with them, but wholly relied on us, it occasioned them

---

4. Action or quality that deserves the appropriate recompense. See *Oxford English Dictionary*, 1st ed., s.v."Desert," n. 1, 2a.
5. This word is now spelled"Narragansett"; this edition follows Winslow's spelling.
6. Probably Wampanoag and Massachusett peoples.

to sleight[7] and brave[8] us with so many threats as they did. At length came one of them to us, who was sent by *Conanacus* their chief *Sachim* or King, accompanied with one *Tokamahamon*[9] a friendly *Indian*. This messenger inquired for *Tisquantum* our Interpreter, who not being at home seemed rather to be glad than sorry, and leaving for him a bundle of new arrows lapped in a rattle Snakes skin, desired to depart with all expedition. But our Governours[10] not knowing what to make of this strange carriage,[11] and comparing it with that we had formerly heard, committed him to the custody of Captain *Standish*,[12] hoping now to know some certainty of that we so often heard, either by his own relation to us, or to *Tisquantum* at his return, desiring my self, having special familiarity with the other fore-named *Indian*,[13] to see if I could learn any thing from him, whose answer was sparingly to this effect; that he could not certainly tell, but thought they were enemies to us. That night Captain *Standish* gave me and another charge of him, and gave us order to use him kindly, and that he should not want any thing he desired, and to take all occasions to talk and inquire of the reasons of those reports we heard, and withal[14] to signify that upon his true relation he should be sure of his own freedom. At first fear so possessed him, that he could scarce say any thing: but in the end became more familiar, and told us that the messenger which his Master[15] sent in Summer to treat of peace, at his return persuaded him rather to war; and to the end he might provoke him thereunto, (as appeared to him by our reports) detained many of the things were sent him by our Governour, scorning the meanness of them both in respect of what himself had formerly sent, & also of the greatness of his own person; so

---

7. To treat with indifference or disrespect. Now spelled "slight." See *Oxford English Dictionary*, 1st ed., s.v. "Slight," v., 3a.

8. To challenge, defy. See *Oxford English Dictionary*, 1st ed., s.v. "Brave," v., 1.

9. *Tokamahamon*, like Tisquantum and Hobbamock, was appointed by Massasoit as an interpreter for the colonists. See *Relation or Journal*, 46, and the excerpt from Winslow's journey to Pokanoket in section 3.

10. William Bradford was governor by this time. Winslow may also have been referring to Isaac Allerton, Bradford's assistant.

11. Manner of carrying, conduct, behavior.

12. Myles Standish was one of the original Plimoth colonists, although he was not a Separatist. He served as a military leader, assistant governor, and treasurer.

13. The Narragansett man.

14. In addition.

15. Conanacus.

that he much blamed the former Messenger, saying, that upon the knowledge of this his false carriage, it would cost him his [3] life; but assured
us that upon his relation of our speech then with him to his Master, he
would be friends with us. Of this we informed the Governour and his
Assistant, and Captain *Standish*, who after consultation considered him
howsoever but in the state of a messenger, and it being as well against
the Law of Arms amongst them as us in *Europe*, to lay violent hands on
any such, set him at liberty, the Governour giving him order to certify his
Master that he had heard of his large and many threatenings, at which
he was much offended, daring him in those respects to the utmost, if he
would not be reconciled to live peaceably as other his neighbors; manifesting withal (as ever) his desire of peace; but his fearless resolution, if he
could not so live amongst them. After which he caused meat to be offered
him, but he refused to eat, making all speed to return, and giving many
thanks for his liberty. But requesting the other *Indian* again to return,
the weather being violent, he used many words to persuade him to stay
longer, but could not. Whereupon he left him, and said he was with his
friends, and would not take a journey in such extremity.

After this when *Tisquantum* returned, and the arrows were delivered,
and the manner of the messengers carriage related, he signified to the
Governour, that to send the rattle Snakes skin in that manner, imported
enmity, and that it was no better than a challenge.[16] Here-upon after
some deliberation, the Governour stuffed the skin with powder and shot,
and sent it back, returning no less defiance to *Conanacus*, assuring him if
he had shipping now present thereby to send his men to *Nanohigganset*
(the place of his abode) they should not need to come so far by land to us:
yet withal shewing that they should never come unwelcome or unlooked
for. This message was sent by an *Indian*, and delivered in such sort, as
it was no small terrour to this savage [4] King, insomuch as he would
not once touch the powder and shot, or suffer it to stay in his house or
Country. Whereupon the Messenger refusing it, another took it up, and
having been posted from place to place a long time, at length came whole
back again.

---

16. See the introduction, note 114 for the possible interpretations of the arrows
wrapped in snakeskin.

In the mean time, knowing our own weakness, notwithstanding our high words and lofty looks towards them, and still lying open to all casualty, having as yet (under God) no other defense than our Arms, we thought it most needful to impale[17] our Town, which with all expedition we accomplished in the month of February and some few days, taking in the top of the Hill under which our Town is seated, making four bulwarks or jetties without the ordinary circuit of the pale,[18] from whence we could defend the whole Town: In three whereof are gates, and the fourth in time to be. This being done, Captain *Standish* divided our strength into four squadrons or companies, appointing whom he thought most fit to have command of each; And at a general Muster or Training, appointed each his place, gave each his Company, giving them charge upon every alarm to resort to their Leaders to their appointed place, and in his absence, to be commanded and directed by them. That done according to his order, each drew his Company to his appointed place for defense, and there together discharged their muskets. After which they brought their new Commanders to their houses, where again they graced them with their shot, and so departed.

Fearing also lest the enemy at any time should take any advantage by firing our houses, Captain *Standish* appointed a certain Company, that whensoever they saw or heard fire to be cried in the Town, should only betake themselves to their Arms, and should [5] enclose the house or place so endangered, and stand aloof on their guard, with their backs towards the fire, to prevent treachery, if any were in that kind intended. If the fire were in any of the houses of this guard, they were then freed from it, but not otherwise, without special command.

Long before this time we promised the people of *Massachuset* in the beginning of March to come unto them, and trade for their Furs, which being then come, we began to make preparation for that voyage. In the mean time, an *Indian* called *Hobbamock*, who still lived in the Town, told us, that he feared the *Massachusets* or *Massachuseucks* (for they so called the people of that place) were joined in confederacy with the

---

17. To enclose with stakes or posts, to fence in. See *Oxford English Dictionary*, 1st ed., s.v. "Impale," v., 1a.

18. A fence or boundary. See *Oxford English Dictionary*, 3rd ed., s.v. "Pale," n.1, I.

Nanohigganneucks, or people of *Nanohigganset*, and that they therefore
would take this opportunity to cut off Captain *Standish* and his company
abroad: but howsoever in the mean time, it was to be feared that the
Nanohigganeuks would assault the Town at home, giving many reasons
for his jealousy, as also that *Tisquantum* was in the confederacy, who we
should find would use many persuasions to draw us from our shallops[19]
to the *Indians* houses for their better advantage. To confirm this his jealousy he told us of many secret passages that passed between him and
others, having their meetings ordinarily abroad in the woods: but if at
home howsoever he was excluded from their secrecy, saying it was the
manner of the *Indians* when they meant plainly to deal openly: but in this
his practise there was no shew of honesty.

   Hereupon the Governour, together with his Assistant and Captain
Standish, called together such, as by them were thought most meet[20] for
advice in so weighty a business, who after consideration hereof came to
this resolution; That as hitherto upon all occasions between them and
us, we had ever manifested undaunted courage and resolution, [6] so it
would not now stand with our safety to mew[21] up our selves in our new-
enclosed town, partly because our Store was almost empty, and therefore must seek out for our daily food, without which we could not long
subsist; but especially for that thereby they would see us dismayed, &
be encouraged to prosecute their malicious purposes, with more eagerness than ever they intended: whereas on the contrary, by the blessing of
God, our fearless carriage might be a means to discourage and weaken
their proceedings. And therefore thought best to proceed in our trading
voyage, making this use of that we heard, to go the better provided, and
use the more carefulness both at home and abroad, leaving the event to
the disposing of the Almighty, whose providence as it had hitherto been
over us for good, so we had now no cause (save our sins) to despair of his
mercy in our preservation and continuance, where we desired rather to
be instruments of good to the Heathens about us, than to give them the
least measure of just offense.

---

   19. A boat used in shallow water.
   20. Suitable, fit.
   21. To shut away; to hide, conceal. See *Oxford English Dictionary*, 3rd ed., s.v. "Mew,"
v.3, I.a.

All things being now in readiness, the forenamed Captain with ten men, accompanied with *Tisquantum* and *Hobbamock,* set forwards for the *Massachusets:* but we had no sooner turned the point of the harbour called the *Gurnets nose*[22] (where being becalmed we let fall our grapnel,[23] to set things to rights, and prepare to row) but there came an Indian of *Tisquantums* family, running to certain of our people that were from home with all eagerness, having his face wounded, and the blood still fresh on the same, calling to them to repair home, oft looking behind him, as if some others had him in chase, saying that at *Namaschet*[24] (a town some fifteen miles from us) there were many of the *Nanohiggansets, Massassowat* our supposed friend, and *Conbatant* our feared enemy,[25] with many others, with a resolution to take advantage on the present opportunity, to assault the town in the Captains absence, affirming that he received the wound in his face for [7] speaking in our behalf, and by sleight escaped, looking oft backward, as if he suspected them to be at hand. This he affirmed again to the Governour, whereupon he gave command that three piece of Ordnance should be made ready and discharged, to the end that if we were not out of hearing, we might return thereat. Which we no sooner heard, but we repaired homeward with all convenient speed, arming our selves, and making all in readiness to fight. When we entered the harbour, we saw the Town likewise on their guard, whither we hasted with all convenient speed. The news being made known unto us, *Hobbamock* said flatly that it was false, assuring us of *Massassowats* faithfulness; howsoever he presumed he would never have undertaken any such act without his privity,[26] himself being a Pniese, that is, one of his chiefest champions or men of valour, it being the manner amongst them not to undertake such enterprises without the advice and furtherance of men of that rank. To this the Governour answered, he should be sorry that any just and necessary occasions of war should arise between him and any [of] the Savages, but especially *Massassowat,* not that he feared him more than the rest,

---

22. Now Gurnet Point, Mass., in Plymouth Harbor.
23. A small anchor.
24. Now part of Middleborough, Mass. See Young, *Chronicles of the Pilgrim Fathers,* 204, n. 4.
25. Conbatant was a Wampanoag sachem under Massasoit. The colonists feared that he was making plans with the Narragansetts to attack them. See *Relation or Journal,* 53.
26. Knowledge of private affairs.

but because his love more exceeded towards him than any. Whereunto *Hobbamock* replied; There was no cause wherefore he should distrust him, and therefore should do well to continue his affections.

But to the end things might be made more manifest, the Governour caused *Hobbamock* to send his wife with all privacy to *Puckanokick*[27] the chief place of *Massassowats* residence, (pretending other occasions) there to inform herself, and so us, of the right state of things. When she came thither, and saw all things quiet, and that no such matter was or had been intended, told *Massassowat* what had happened at *Plimoth*, (by them called *Patuxet*) which when he understood, he [8] was much offended at the carriage of *Tisquantum*, returning many thanks to the Governour for his good thoughts of him; and assuring him that according to their first Articles of peace, he would send word and give warning when any such business was towards.[28]

Thus by degrees we began to discover *Tisquantum*, whose ends were only to make himself great in the eyes of this Country-men, by means of his nearness and favour with us, not caring who fell so he stood. In the general, his course was to persuade them he could lead us to peace or war at his pleasure, and would oft threaten the *Indians*, sending them word in a private manner, we were intended shortly to kill them, that thereby he might get gifts to himself to work their peace, insomuch as they had him in greater esteem than many of their *Sachims*; yea they themselves sought to him, who promised them peace in respect of us; yea and protection also, so as they would resort to him. So that whereas diverse were wont to rely on *Massassowat* for protection, and resort to his abode, now they began to leave him, and seek after *Tisquantum*. Now though he could not make good these his large promises, especially because of the continued peace between *Massassowat* and us, he therefore raised this false alarm, hoping whilst things were hot in the heat of blood, to provoke us to march into his Country against him, whereby he hoped to kindle such a flame as would not easily be quenched, and hoping if that block were once removed, there were no other between him and honour; which he loved as his life, and preferred before his peace. For these and the like abuses,

---

27. Puckanokick or Pokanoket was located roughly in what are now Bristol and Warren, R.I.
28. Approaching. See section 3 for these "Articles of peace."

the Governour sharply reproved him, yet was he so necessary and profit-able an instrument, as at that time we could not miss him. But when we understood his dealings, we certified all the *Indians* of our ignorance and innocence therein, assuring [9] them till they begun with us, they should have no cause to fear. And if any hereafter should raise any such reports, they should punish them as liars and seekers of their and our disturbance, which gave the *Indians* good satisfaction on all sides.

After this we proceeded in our voyage to the *Massachusets*, where we had good store of Trade, and (blessed be God) returned in safety, though driven from before our Town in great danger and extremity of weather.

At our return, we found *Massassowat* at the Plantation, who made his seeming just Apology for all former matters of accusation, being much of-fended and enraged against *Tisquantum*, whom the Governour pacified as much as he could for the present. But not long after his departure, he sent a messenger to the Governour, entreating him to give way to the death of *Tisquantum*, who had so much abused him. But the Governour answered; Although he had deserved to die both in respect of him and us; yet for our sakes he desired he would spare him, and the rather because without him he knew not well how to understand himself, or any other the *Indians*. With this answer the messenger returned, but came again not long after, accompanied with diverse others, demanding him from *Massassowat* their Master, as being one of his subjects, whom by our first Articles of peace we could not retain: yet because he would not willingly do it without the Governours approbation, offered him many Beavers skins for his consent thereto, saying, that according to their manner, their *Sachim* had sent his own knife, and them therewith, to cut off his head and hands, and bring them to him. To which the Governour answered; It was not the manner of the *English* to sell mens lives at a price, but [10] when they had deserved justly to die, to give them their reward, and therefore refused their Beavers as a gift: but sent for *Tisquantum*, who though he knew their intent, yet offered not to fly, but came and accused *Hobbamock* as the author and worker of his overthrow; yielding himself to the Governour to be sent or not according as he thought meet. But at the instant, when our Gover-nour was ready to deliver him into the hands of his Executioners, a Boat was seen at Sea to cross before our Town, and fall behind a head-land not far off: whereupon, having heard many rumors of the *French*, and not knowing whether there were any combination between the Savages and them, the Governour told the *Indians*, he would first know what Boat that was ere[29] he would deliver him into their custody. But being mad with rage, and impatient at delay, they departed in great heat.

Here let me not omit one notable (though wicked) practise of this *Tisquantum*, who to the end he might possess his Countrymen with the greater fear of us, and so consequently of himself, told them we had the plague buried in our store-house, which at our pleasure we could send forth to what place or people we would, and destroy them therewith, though we stirred not from home. Being upon the fore-named brabbles[30] sent for by the Governour to this place, where *Hobbamock* was and some other of us, the ground being broke in the middest of the house, (whereunder certain barrels of powder were buried, though unknown to him) *Hobbamock* asked him what it meant? To whom he readily answered; That was the place wherein the plague was buried, whereof he formerly told him and others. After this *Hobbamock* asked one of our people, whether such a thing were, and whether we had such [11] command of it? Who answered no; But the God of the English had it in store, and could send it at his pleasure to the destruction of his and our enemies.

This was, as I take it, about the end of May 1622. At which time our store of victuals was wholly spent, having lived long before with a bare and short allowance: The reason was, that supply of men before mentioned, which came so unprovided, not landing so much as a barrel of bread or meal for their whole company, but contrariwise received from us for their ships store homeward. Neither were the setters forth thereof altogether to be blamed therein, but rather certain amongst our selves, who were too prodigal in their writing and reporting of that plenty we enjoyed.[31] But that I may return.

This Boat proved to be a Shallop that belonged to a fishing ship, called the Sparrow, set forth by Master *Thomas Weston*, late Merchant and Citizen of London, which brought six or seven passengers at his charge, that should before have been landed at our Plantation, who also brought

---

29. Before.
30. Dispute.
31. Winslow probably refers to his own glowing report of New England in 1622. See the introduction and the excerpt from the *Relation or Journal* in section 3.

no more provision for the present than served the Boats gang for their return to the ship, which made her voyage at a place called *Damarins Cove* near *Munhiggen*[32] some forty leagues from us North-east-ward; about which place there fished above thirty sail of ships, and whither my self was employed by our Governour, with orders to take up such victuals as the ships could spare, where I found kind entertainment and good respect, with a willingness to supply our wants: But being not able to spare that quantity I required, by reason of the necessity of some amongst themselves, whom they supplied before my coming, would not take any Bills for the same, but did what they could freely, wishing their store had been such as they might in [12] greater measure have expressed their own love, and supplied our necessities, for which they sorrowed, provoking one another to the utmost of their abilities: which although it were not much amongst so many people as were at the Plantation, yet through the provident and discreet care of the Governours, recovered and preserved strength till our own crop on the ground was ready.

Having dispatched there, I returned home with all speed convenient, where I found the state of the Colony much weaker than when I left it: for till now we were never without some bread, the want whereof much abated the strength and flesh of some, and swelled others. But here it may be said, if the Country abound with Fish and Fowl in such measure as is reported, how could men undergo such measure of hardness, except through their own negligence? I answer; Every thing must be expected in its proper season. No man, as one saith, will go into an Orchard in the Winter to gather Cherries: so he that looks for Fowl there in the Summer, will be deceived in his expectation. The time they continue in plenty with us, is from the beginning of October to the end of March: but these extremities befell us in May and June. I confess that as the Fowl decrease, so Fish increase. And indeed their exceeding abundance was a great cause of increasing our wants. For though our Bay and Creeks were full of Bass, and other fish, yet for want of fit and strong Saynes,[33] and other netting, they for the most part break through and carried all away

32. The Damariscove islands, near Monhegan, Me. See Young, *Chronicles of the Pilgrim Fathers*, 278, n. 2.

33. A fishing net. Now spelled seines. See *Oxford English Dictionary*, 1st ed., s.v. "Seine," n.I, Ia.

before them. And though the Sea were full of Cod, yet we had neither tackling nor harseis[34] for our Shallops. And indeed had we not been in a place where diverse sorts of shell-fish are that may be taken with the hand, we must have perished, unless God had raised [13] some unknown or extraordinary means for our preservation.

In the time of these straits (indeed before my going to *Munhiggen*) the *Indians* began again to cast forth many insulting speeches, glorying in our weakness, and giving out how easy it would be ere long to cut us off. Now also *Massassowat* seemed to frown on us, and neither came or sent to us as formerly. These things occasioned further thoughts of Fortification: And whereas we have a Hill called the Mount, enclosed within our pale, under which our Town is seated, we resolved to erect a Fort thereon, from whence a few might easily secure the Town from any assault the *Indians* can make, whilst the rest might be employed as occasion served. This work was begun with great eagerness, and with the approbation of all men, hoping that this being once finished, and a continual guard there kept, it would utterly discourage the Savages from having any hopes or thoughts of rising against us. And though it took the greatest part of our strength from dressing our corn, yet (life being continued) we hoped God would raise some means in stead thereof for our further preservation.

In the end of June, or beginning of July, came into our harbour two ships of Master *Westons* aforesaid, the one called the *Charitie*, the other the *Swan*, having in them some fifty or sixty men sent over at his own charge to plant for him. These we received into our Town, affording them whatsoever courtesy our mean condition could afford. There the *Charitie*, being the bigger ship, left them, having many passengers which she was to land in *Virginia*. In the mean time, the body of them refreshed themselves at *Plimoth*, whilst some most fit sought out a place for them. That little store of corn we had, [14] was exceedingly wasted by the unjust and dishonest walking[35] of these strangers, who though they would sometimes seem to help us in our labour about our corn, yet spared not day and night to steal the same, it being then eatable, and pleasant to taste, though

---

34. Possibly a variation of "harry-water" net, "A kind of net with meshes so small as to catch very small fish." *Oxford English Dictionary*, 1st ed., s.v. "Harry-water," adj., 1.
35. Behavior.

green and unprofitable. And though they received much kindness, set light both by it and us; not sparing to requite the love we shewed them, with secret backbitings, revilings, &c. the chief of them being forestalled[36] and made against us, before they came, as after appeared: Nevertheless for their Masters[37] sake, who formerly had deserved well from us, we continued to do them whatsoever good or furtherance we could, attributing these things to the want of conscience and discretion, expecting each day, when God in his providence would disburden us of them, sorrowing that their Over-seers were not of more ability and fitness for their places, and much fearing what would be the issue of such raw and unconscionable beginnings.

At length their Coasters[38] returned, having found in their judgment a place fit for plantation, within the Bay of the *Massachusets,* at a place called by the Indians *Wichaguscusset.*[39] To which place the body of them went with all convenient speed, leaving still with us such as were sick and lame, by the Governours permission, though on their parts undeserved, whom our Surgeon[40] by the help of God recovered gratis for them, and they fetched home, as occasion served.

They had not been long from us, ere the Indians filled our ears with clamours against them, for stealing their corn, and other abuses conceived by them. At which we grieved the more, because the same men, in mine own hearing, had been earnest in persuading Captain *Standish,* before their coming to solicit our [15] Governour to send some of his men to plant by them, alleging many reasons how it might be commodious for us. But we knew no means to redress those abuses, save reproof, and advising them to better walking, as occasion served.

In the end of *August* came other two ships into our harbour, the one (as I take it) was called the *Discoverie,* Captain *Jones* having the command thereof, the other was that ship of Mr. *Westons* called the *Sparrow,* which had now made her voyage of fish, and was consorted with the other, being both bound for *Virginia.* Of Captain *Jones* we furnished our selves of such

---

36. Prejudiced or inclined against.
37. Thomas Weston.
38. Those who sailed along the coast.
39. Now Weymouth, Mass. This word is now usually spelled Wessagusset.
40. Samuel Fuller.

provisions as we most needed, and he could best spare, who as he used us kindly, so made us pay largely for the things we had. And had not the Almighty, in his All-ordering Providence, directed him to us, it would have gone worse with us, than ever it had been, or after was: for, as we had now but small store of corn for the year following: so for want of supply, we were worn out of all manner of trucking[41] stuff, not having any means left to help our selves by trade; but, through Gods good mercy towards us, he had wherewith, and did supply our wants on that kind competently.

In the end of *September,* or beginning of *October,* Mr. *Westons* biggest ship called the *Charitie,* returned for *England,* and left their Colony sufficiently victualed, as some of most credit amongst them reported. The lesser, called the *Swan,* remained with his Colony for their further help. At which time they desired to join in partnership with us to trade for corn; to which our Governour and his Assistant agreed upon such equal conditions, as were drawn and confirmed between them and us. The chief places aimed at were to the Southward of *Cape Cod,* and the more because *Tisquantum,* whose peace before this time [16] was wrought with *Massassowat,* undertook to discover unto us that supposed, and still hoped passage within the Sholes.[42]

Both Colonies being thus agreed, and their companies fitted and joined together, we resolved to set forward, but were oft crossed in our purposes; as first Master *Richard Greene,* brother in Law to Master *Weston,* who from him had a charge in the oversight and government of his Colony, died suddenly at our Plantation, to whom we gave burial befitting his place, in the best manner we could. Afterward, having further order to proceed by letter from their other Governour at the *Massachusets,* twice Captain *Standish* set forth with them, but were driven in again by cross and violent winds: himself the second time being sick of a violent fever. By reason whereof (our own wants being like to be now greater than formerly; partly, because we were enforced to neglect our corn, and spend much time in fortification, but especially because such havoc was made of that little we had, through the unjust and dishonest carriage of those people before mentioned, at our first entertainment of them) our Gov-

41. Trading.
42. Shallow water.

ernour in his own person supplied the Captains place, and in the month
of *November* again set forth, having *Tisquantum* for his Interpreter and
Pilot, who affirmed he had twice passed within the Sholes of *Cape Cod*,
both with *English* and *French*. Nevertheless, they went so far with him, as
the Master of the ship saw no hope of passage: but being (as he thought)
in danger, bear up, and according to *Tisquantums* directions, made for an
harbour not far from them, at a place called *Manamoycke*,[43] which they
found, and sounding it with their shallop found the channel, though but
narrow and crooked, where at length they harboured the ship. Here they
perceived that the tide set in and out with more violence at some [17]
other place more Southerly, which they had not seen nor could discover,
by reason of the violence of the season all the time of their abode there.
Some judged the entrance thereof might be beyond the Sholes, but there
is no certainty thereof as yet known. That night the Governour accompanied with others, having *Tisquantum* for his Interpreter went ashore;
At first the Inhabitants played least in sight, because none of our people
had ever been there before; but understanding the ends of their coming,
at length came to them, welcoming our Governour according to their
Savage manner, refreshing them very well with store of venison and other
victuals, which they brought them in great abundance, promising to trade
with them, with a seeming gladness of the occasion: yet their joy was
mixed with much jealousy, as appeared by their after practises: for at first
they were loath their dwellings should be known, but when they saw our
Governours resolution to stay on the shore all night, they brought him
to their houses, having first conveyed all their stuff to a remote place,
not far from the same, which one of our men walking forth occasionally
espied; whereupon, on the sudden, neither it nor them could be found,
and so many times after upon conceived occasions, they would be all
gone, bag and baggage: But being afterwards (by *Tisquantums* means)
better persuaded, they left their jealousy and traded with them; where
they got eight hogsheads[44] of corn and beans, though the people were
but few. This gave our Governour and the company good encouragement. *Tisquantum* being still confident in the passage, and the Inhabitants

---

43. Now Chatham, Mass. See Young, *Chronicles of the Pilgrim Fathers*, 300, n. 1.
44. A large cask.

affirming, they had seen ships of good burden pass within the Sholes
aforesaid. But here, though they had determined to make a second assay,[45]
yet God had otherways disposed, who struck *Tisquantum* with sickness,
in so much as he [18] there died, which crossed their Southward trading,
and the more because the Masters sufficiency was much doubted, and
the season very tempestuous, and not fit to go upon discovery, having no
guide to direct them.

From thence they departed, and the wind being fair for the *Massachusets*
went thither, and the rather because the Savages upon our motion had
planted much corn for us, which they promised not long before that time.
When they came thither, they found a great sickness to be amongst the
Indians, not unlike the plague, if not the same. They renewed their complaints to our Governour, against that other plantation seated by them,
for their injurious walking. But indeed the trade both for Furs and corn
was overthrown in that place, they giving as much for a quart of corn,
as we used to do for a Beavers skin; so that little good could be there
done. From thence they returned into the bottom of the Bay of Cape
Cod, to a place called *Nauset*, where the *Sachim* used the Governour very
kindly, and where they bought eight or ten hogsheads of corn and beans.[46]
Also at a place called *Mattachiest*,[47] where they had like kind entertainment and corn also. During the time of their trade in these places, there
were so great and violent storms, as the ship was much endangered, and
our shallop cast away, so that they had now no means to carry the corn
aboard that they had bought, the ship riding by their report well near two
leagues from the same, her own Boat being small, and so leaky, (having no
Carpenter with them) as they durst[48] scarce fetch wood or water in her.
Hereupon the Governour caused the corn to be made in a round stack,
and bought mats, and cut sedge to cover it, and gave charge to the *Indians*

---

45. Attempt.
46. Nauset is near what is now Eastham, Mass; the colonists referred to the sachem
there as Iyanough, describing him as "man not exceeding twenty-six years of age, but
very personable, gentle, courteous, and fair condition, indeed not like a Savage, save for
his attire; his entertainment was answerable to his parts, and his cheer plentiful and
various." See *Relation or Journal*, 50; and, on Nauset's location, Young, *Chronicles of the
Pilgrim Fathers*, 216, n. 1.
47. Between Barnstable and Yarmouth harbors, Mass. See Young, *Chronicles of the
Pilgrim Fathers*, 215, n. 1.
48. Dared.

not to meddle with it, promising him that dwelt next to it a reward, if he would keep vermin also from it, which he undertook, and the [19] *Sachim* promised to make good. In the mean time, according to the Governours request, the *Sachim* sent men to seek the shallop, which they found buried almost in sand at a high-water mark, having many things remaining in her, but unserviceable for the present; whereof the Governour gave the *Sachim* special charge that it should not be further broken, promising ere long to fetch both it and the corn; assuring them, if neither were diminished, he would take it as a sign of their honest and true friendship, which they so much made shew of, but if they were, they should certainly smart for their unjust and dishonest dealing, and further make good whatsoever they had so taken. So he did likewise at *Mattachiest*, and took leave of them, being resolved to leave the ship, and take his journey home by land with our own company, sending word to the ship, that they should take their first opportunity to go for *Plimoth*, where he determined, by the permission of God, to meet them. And having procured a Guide, it being no less than fifty miles to our Plantation, set forward, receiving all respect that could be from the *Indians* in his journey, and came safely home, though weary and surbated,[49] whither some three days after the ship also came. The corn being divided which they had got, Master *Westons* company went to their own Plantation, it being further agreed, that they should return with all convenient speed, and bring their Carpenter, that they might fetch the rest of the corn, and save the shallop.

At their return, Captain *Standish* being recovered and in health, took another shallop, and went with them to the corn, which they found in safety as they left it: also they mended the other shallop, and got all their corn aboard the ship. This was in January, as I take it, it being very cold and stormy, insomuch as (the harbour being none of the best) they were constrained to cut both the shallops from the ships stern, [20] and so lost them both a second time. But the storm being over, and seeking out, they found them both, not having received any great hurt. Whilst they were at *Nauset*, having occasion to lie on the shore, laying their shallop in a Creek not far from them, an *Indian* came into the same, and stole certain Beads, Cissers,[50] and other trifles out of the same, which when the

---

49. Tired from traveling on foot.
50. An early spelling for scissors.

Captain missed, he took certain of his company with him, and went to the *Sachim*, telling him what had happened, and requiring the same again, or the party that stole them, (who was known to certain of the *Indians*) or else he would revenge it on them before his departure, and so took leave for that night being late, refusing whatsoever kindness they offered. On the morrow, the *Sachim* came to their rendezvous, accompanied with many men, in a stately manner, who saluting the Captain in this wise; He thrust out his tongue, that one might see the root thereof, and therewith licked his hand from the wrist to the fingers end, withal bowing the knee, striving to imitate the English gesture, being instructed therein formerly by *Tisquantum*: his men did the like, but in so rude and savage a manner, as our men could scarce forbear to break out in open laughter. After salutation, he delivered the Beads, & other things, to the Captain, saying, he had much beaten the party for doing it, causing the women to make bread, and bring them, according to their desire, seeming to be very sorry for the fact, but glad to be reconciled. So they departed, and came home in safety; where the corn was equally divided, as before.

After this the Governour went to two other inland Towns, with another company, and bought corn likewise of them, the one is called *Namasket*, the other *Manomet*.[51] That from *Namasket* was brought home partly by *Indian* women; but a great sickness arising amongst them, our own men were enforced to fetch [21] home the rest. That at *Manomet* the Governour left in the *Sachims* custody: this Town lieth from us South well near twenty miles, and stands upon a fresh river, which runneth into the Bay of *Nanohigganset*, and cannot be less than sixty miles from thence. It will bear a boat of eight or ten ton to this place. Hither the Dutch or French, or both use to come. It is from hence to the Bay of Cape Cod about eight miles; out of which Bay it floweth into a Creek some six miles almost direct towards the Town. The heads of the River, and this Creek are not far distant. This River yieldeth thus high, Oysters, Mussels, Clams, and other shell-fish, one in shape like a bean, another like a Clam, both good meat, and great abundance at all times; besides it aboundeth with diverse sorts of fresh fish in their seasons. The Governour or *Sachim* of this

---

51. Young identifies Manomet as the part of present-day Sandwich, Mass., located on the Manomet River. See *Chronicles of the Pilgrim Fathers*, 305, n. 1.

place, was called *Canacum*, who had formerly, as well as many others, (yea all with whom as yet we had to do) acknowledged themselves the subjects of our Sovereign Lord the King. This *Sachim* used the Governour very kindly, and it seemed was of good respect and authority amongst the *Indians*. For whilst the Governour was there within night in bitter weather, came two men from *Manamoick*[52] before spoken of, and having set aside their bows and quivers, according to their manner, sat down by the fire, and took a pipe of Tobacco, not using any words in that time, nor any other to them, but all remained silent, expecting when they would speak: At length they looked toward *Canacum*, and one of them made a short speech, and delivered a present to him from his *Sachim*, which was a basket of Tobacco, and many Beads,[53] which the other received thankfully. After which he made a long speech to him, the contents hereof was related to us by *Hobbamock* (who then accompanied the Governour for his Guide) to be as followeth; It happened that two of their men fell out as they were in game[54] (for they [22] use gaming as much as any where, and will play away all, even their skin from their backs, yea and for their wives skins also, though it may be they are many miles distant from them, as my self have seen) and growing to great heat, the one killed the other. The actor of this fact was a *Powah*, one of special note amongst them, and such an one as they could not well miss, yet another people greater than themselves threatened them with war, if they would not put him to death. The party offending was in hold, neither would their *Sachim* do one way or other till their return, resting upon him for advice and furtherance in

52. Winslow previously spelled this word "Manamoycke."
53. These beads are probably *wampumpeag*, or wampum. Fashioned by hand out of the quahog shell, the beads were used to make belts that were part of what Lisa Brooks has called a "spatialized writing tradition." Wampum served as mnemonic devices, as messages and authentications of words, and as symbols of relationships; it reminded people of past events and solidified new connections. In the mid-seventeenth century, colonists exchanged wampum for the furs they desired, and the wampum-fur trade drove up the value of wampum and gave it new meanings as currency. Access to wampum and trade networks was one of the factors in the Pequot War of 1637. See Brooks, *Common Pot*, 10–12 (quotation on 12) and 54–59; Bragdon, *Native People*, 96–98; and Murray, *Indian Giving*, chap. 5.
54. Several colonists describe Natives' "games" or gambling. Roger Williams described the Narragansetts' games, including one he compared to an English card game played with rushes rather than cards and another in which stones were used like dice. See Williams, *Key into the Language*, 169–72.

so weighty a matter. After this there was silence a short time; at length men gave their judgment what they thought best. Amongst others, he asked *Hobbamock* what he thought? Who answered, he was but a stranger to them, but thought it was better that one should die than many, since he had deserved it, and the rest were innocent; whereupon he passed the sentence of death upon him.

Not long after (having no great quantity of corn left) Captain *Standish* went again with a shallop to *Mattachiest*, meeting also with the like extremity of weather, both of wind, snow, and frost, insomuch as they were frozen in the harbour the first night they entered the same. Here they pretended[55] their wonted[56] love, and spared them a good quantity of corn to confirm the same: Strangers also came to this place, pretending only to see him and his company, whom they never saw before that time, but intending to join with the rest to kill them, as after appeared. But being forced through extremity to lodge in their houses, which they much pressed, God possessed the heart of the Captain with just jealousy, giving straight command, that as one part of his company slept, the rest should wake, declaring some things to them which he understood, whereof he could make no [23] good construction. Some of the *Indians* spying a fit opportunity, stole some beads also from him, which he no sooner perceived, having not above six men with him, drew them all from the Boat, and set them on their guard about the *Sachims* house, where the most of the people were, threatening to fall upon them without further delay, if they would not forthwith restore them, signifying to the *Sachim* especially, and so to them all, that as he would not offer the least injury; so he would not receive any at their hands, which should escape without punishment or due satisfaction. Hereupon the *Sachim* bestirred him to find out the party, which when he had done, caused him to return them again to the shallop, and came to the Captain, desiring him to search whether they were not about the Boat, who suspecting their knavery, sent one, who found them lying openly upon the Boats cuddy;[57] yet to appease his anger, they brought corn afresh to trade, insomuch as he laded his shallop, and so departed. This accident so daunted their courage, as they durst not attempt

---

55. Claimed or asserted.
56. Customary, usual.
57. A room in a ship in which the officers and cabin-passengers take their meals.

any thing against him. So that through the good mercy and providence of God they returned in safety. At this place the *Indians* get abundance of Bass both summer and winter: for it being now February they abounded with them.

In the beginning of March, having refreshed himself, he took a shallop, and went to *Manomet*, to fetch home that which the Governour had formerly bought, hoping also to get more from them, but was deceived in his expectation, not finding that entertainment he found else-where, and the Governour had there received. The reason whereof, and of the treachery intended in the place before spoken of, was not then known unto us, but afterwards: wherein may be observed the abundant mercies of God working with his providence for our good. Captain *Standish* being now far [24] from the Boat, and not above two or three of our men with him, and as many with the shallop, was not long at *Canacum* the *Sachims* house, but in came two of the *Massachuset* men, the chief of them was called *Wituwamat*,[58] a notable insulting villain, one who had formerly imbrued his hands in the blood of *English* and *French*, and had oft boasted of his own valour, and derided their weakness, especially because (as he said) they died crying, making sour faces, more like children than men. This villain took a dagger from about his neck, (which he had gotten of Master *Westons* people) and presented it to the *Sachim*, and after made a long speech in an audacious manner, framing it in such sort, as the Captain (though he be the best Linguist amongst us) could not gather any thing from it. The end of it was afterward discovered to be as followeth: The *Massacheuseucks* had formerly concluded to ruinate[59] Master *Westons* Colony, and thought themselves, being about thirty or forty men strong, enough to execute the same: yet they durst not attempt it, till such time as they had gathered more strength to themselves to make their party good against us at *Plimoth*, concluding, that if we remained, (though they had no other Arguments to use against us) yet we would never leave the death of our Countrymen unrevenged, and therefore their safety could not be without the overthrow of both Plantations. To this end they had formerly solicited this *Sachim*, as also the other called *Ianough* at *Mattachiest*, and

---

58. Wituwamat was a Massachusett leader, probably a pniese.

59. To overthrow, but also to throw into poverty, or deprive of moral or social standing. See *Oxford English Dictionary*, 3rd ed., s.v. "Ruinate," v., 1.

many others to assist them, and now again came to prosecute the same; and since there was so fair an opportunity offered by the Captains presence, they thought best to make sure him and his company. After this his message was delivered, his entertainment much exceeded the Captains, insomuch as he scorned at their behaviour, and told them of it: after which they would have persuaded him, [25] because the weather was cold, to have sent to the Boat for the rest of his company, but he would not, desiring according to promise, that the corn might be carried down, and he would content the women for their labour, which they did. At the same time there was a lusty *Indian* of *Paomet* or *Cape Cod*[60] then present, who had ever demeaned[61] himself well towards us, being in his general carriage, very affable, courteous, and loving, especially towards the Captain. This Savage was now entered into confederacy with the rest, yet to avoid suspicion, made many signs of his continued affections, and would needs bestow a kettle of some six or seven gallons on him, and would not accept of any thing in lieu thereof, saying, he was rich, and could afford to bestow such favours on his friends whom he loved: also he would freely help to carry some of the corn, affirming he had never done the like in his life before, and the wind being bad would needs lodge with him at their Rendezvous, having indeed undertaken to kill him before they parted, which done they intended to fall upon the rest. The night proved exceeding cold, insomuch as the Captain could not take any rest, but either walked or turned himself to and fro at the fire: This the other observed, and asked wherefore he did not sleep as at other times, who answered he knew not well, but had no desire at all to rest. So that he then missed his opportunity. The wind serving on the next day, they returned home, accompanied with the other *Indian*, who used many arguments to persuade them to go to *Paomet*, where himself had much corn, and many other, the most whereof he would procure for us, seeming to sorrow for our wants. Once the Captain put forth with him, and was forced back by contrary wind; which wind serving for the *Massachuset*, was fitted to go thither. But on a sudden it altered again.

60. Young suggests that Paomet corresponds to Truro, Mass. See Young, *Chronicles of the Pilgrim Fathers*, 311, n. 3.
61. Behaved.

During the time that the Captain was at *Manomet*, news came to *Plimoth*, that *Massassowat* was like to die, and that at the same time there was a Dutch ship driven so [26] high on the shore by stress of weather, right before his dwelling, that till the tides increased, she could not be got off. Now it being a commendable manner of the Indians, when any (especially of note) are dangerously sick, for all that profess friendship to them, to visit them in their extremity, either in their persons, or else to send some acceptable persons to them, therefore it was thought meet (being a good and warrantable action) that as we had ever professed friendship, so we should now maintain the same, by observing this their laudable custom: and the rather, because we desired to have some conference with the Dutch, not knowing when we should have so fit an opportunity. To that end my self having formerly been there, and understanding in some measure the Dutch tongue, the Governour again laid this service upon my self, and fitted me with some cordials to administer to him, having one Master *John Hamden* a Gentleman of *London* (who then wintered with us, and desired much to see the Country) for my Consort,[62] and *Hobbamock* for our guide. So we set forward, and lodged the first night at *Namasket*, where we had friendly entertainment. The next day about one of the clock, we came to a ferry in *Conbatants* Country, where upon discharge of my piece, diverse Indians came to us from a house not far off. There they told us, that *Massassowat* was dead, and that day buried, and that the Dutch would be gone before we could get thither, having hove[63] off their ship already. This news struck us blank: but especially *Hobbamock*, who desired we might return with all speed. I told him I would first think of it, considering now that he being dead, *Conbatant* was the most like to succeed him, and that we were not above three miles from *Mattapuyst*[64] his dwelling place, although he were but a hollow-hearted friend towards us, I thought no time so fit as this, to enter into more friendly terms with him, and the rest of the *Sachims* thereabout, hoping (through the blessing of God) it would be a means in that unsettled state,

---

62. John Hamden lived temporarily in New England; he was a member of the English Parliament in the 1640s. See Russell, "John Hampden (1595–1643)."

63. Departed by sea.

64. Also spelled Mattapoiset, near what is now called Gardner's Neck in Swansea, Mass. See Young, *Chronicles of the Pilgrim Fathers*, 315, n. 3.

to settle their affections towards us, and though it were [27] somewhat
dangerous, in respect of our personal safety, because my self and *Hobbamock* had been employed upon a service against him, which he might now
fitly revenge,[65] yet esteeming it the best means, leaving the event to God
in his mercy, I resolved to put it in practise, if Master *Hamden* and
Hobbamock durst attempt it with me, whom I found willing to that or any
other course might tend to the general good. So we went towards
Mattapuyst. In the way, *Hobbamock* manifesting a troubled spirit, broke
forth into these speeches, *Neen womasu Sagimus, neen womasu Sagimus,*
&c. My loving *Sachim,* my loving *Sachim.* Many have I known, but never
any like thee: And turning him to me said; Whilst I lived, I should never
see his like amongst the *Indians,* saying, he was no liar, he was not bloody
and cruel like other *Indians;* In anger and passion he was soon reclaimed,
easy to be reconciled towards such as had offended him, ruled by reason
in such measure, as he would not scorn the advice of mean men, and that
he governed his men better with few strokes than others did with many;
truly loving where he loved; yea he feared we had not a faithful friend left
among the *Indians,* shewing how he oft-times restrained their malice, &c.
continuing a long speech with such signs of lamentation and unfeigned
sorrow, as it would have made the hardest heart relent. At length we came
to *Mattapuyst,* and went to the *Sachimo Comaco* (for so they call the
Sachims place, though they call an ordinary house *Witeo*) but *Conbatant*
the *Sachim* was not at home, but at *Puckanokick,* which was some five or
six miles off; the *Squa-sachim*[66] (for so they call the *Sachims* wife) gave us
friendly entertainment. Here we inquired again concerning *Massassowat,*
they thought him dead, but knew no certainty; whereupon I hired one to
go with all expedition to *Puckanokick* that we might know the certainty
thereof, and withal to acquaint *Conbatant* with our there being. About
half an hour before Sun-setting, the messenger returned, and told us that

---

65. Winslow may be referring to an incident in which the colonists heard that Combatant (also spelled Coubatant) had decided to align with the Narragansetts against
Massasoit and had taken Tisquantum captive. The colonists responded by traveling to
Combatant's village, firing their guns into the air, and retaking Tisquantum. See *Relation
or Journal,* 53–55.

66. The word "Squa-sachim" is a pidgin, created after colonization as colonists and
Natives developed strategies for communicating. The Massachusett word for a female
leader is *sonkusq.* See Goddard, "Use of Pidgins and Jargons," 72.

he was not yet dead, though there was no hope [28] we should find him living. Upon this we were much revived, and set forward with all speed, though it was late within night ere we got thither. About two of the clock that afternoon the Dutchmen departed, so that in that respect our journey was frustrate. When we came thither, we found the house so full of men, as we could scarce get in, though they used their best diligence to make way for us. There were they in the middest of their charms for him, making such a hellish noise, as it distempered us that were well, and therefore unlike to ease him that was sick. About him were six or eight women, who chafed his arms, legs, and thighs, to keep heat in him; when they had made an end of their charming, one told him that his friends the *English* were come to see him; (having understanding left, but his sight was wholly gone) he asked who was come, they told him *Winsnow* (for they cannot pronounce the letter l, but ordinarily n in the place thereof) he desired to speak with me; when I came to him, and they told him of it, he put forth his hand to me, which I took; then he said twice, though very inwardly, *keen Winsnow*, which is to say, Art though *Winslow?* I answered, *ahhe* that is, yes; then he doubled these words, *Matta neen wonckanet namen Winsnow*; that is to say, O *Winslow I shall never see thee again.*[67] Then I called *Hobbamock* and desired him to tell *Massassowat*, that the Governour hearing of his sickness was sorry for the same, and though by reason of many businesses he could not come himself, yet he sent me with such things for him as he thought most likely to do him good in this his extremity, and whereof if he pleased to take, I would presently give him; which he desired, and having a confection of many comfortable[68] conserves, &c. on the point of my knife, I gave him some, which I could scarce get through his teeth; when it was dissolved in his mouth, he swallowed the juice of it, whereat those that were about him much rejoiced, saying, he had not swallowed any thing in two days before. Then I desired to see his mouth, which was exceedingly furred, and [29] his tongue swelled in such manner, as it was not possible for him to eat such meat as they had, his passage being stopped up: then I washed his mouth, and scraped his tongue, and got abundance of corruption out of the same.

---

67. Goddard points out that the literal translation of this phrase is: "not I again see Winslow." See ibid.

68. Strengthening, refreshing to the body.

After which, I gave him more of the confection, which he swallowed with more readiness; then he desiring to drink, I dissolved some of it in water, and gave him thereof: within half an hour this wrought a great alteration in him in the eyes of all that beheld him; presently after his sight began to come to him, which gave him and us good encouragement. In the mean time I inquired how he slept, and when he went to the stool? They said he slept not in two days before, and had not had a stool in five; then I gave him more, and told him of a mishap we had by the way in breaking a bottle of drink, which the Governour also sent him, saying, if he would send any of his men to *Patuxet,* I would send for more of the same, also for chickens to make him broth, and for other things which I knew were good for him, and would stay the return of the messenger if he desired. This he took marvelous kindly, and appointed some who were ready to go by two of the clock in the morning, against which time I made ready a letter, declaring therein our good success, the state of his body, &c. desiring to send me such things as I sent for, and such physic as the Surgeon durst administer to him. He requested me that the day following, I would take my Piece, and kill him some Fowl, and make him some English pottage, such as he had eaten at *Plimoth,* which I promised: after his stomach coming to him, I must needs make him some without Fowl, before I went abroad, which somewhat troubled me, being unaccustomed and unacquainted in such businesses, especially having nothing to make it comfortable, my Consort being as ignorant as my self; but being we must do somewhat, I caused a woman to bruise some corn, and take the flower[69] from it, and set over the grut[70] or broken corn in a pipkin (for they have earthen pots of all sizes.) [30] When the day broke, we went out (it being now March) to seek herbs, but could not find any but strawberry leaves, of which I gathered a handful and put into the same, and because I had nothing to relish[71] it, I went forth again, and pulled up a Saxafras[72] root, and sliced a piece thereof, and boiled it till it had a good relish, and then took it out again. The broth being boiled, I strained it through my hand-

---

69. Winslow may mean "flour" here.
70. This word is etymologically related to "grit." See *Oxford English Dictionary,* 1st ed., s.v. "Groot," n.
71. To give flavor.
72. Sassafras.

kerchief, and gave him at least a pint, which he drank, and liked it very well. After this his sight mended more and more, also he had three moderate stools, and took some rest. Insomuch as we with admiration blessed God for giving his blessing to such raw and ignorant means, making no doubt of his recovery, himself and all of them acknowledging us the instruments of his preservation. That morning he caused me to spend in going from one to another amongst those that were sick in the Town, requesting me to wash their mouths also, and give to each of them some of the same I gave him, saying, they were good folk. This pains I took with willingness, though it were much offensive to me, not being accustomed with such poisonous savours.[73] After dinner he desired me to get him a Goose or Duck, and make him some pottage therewith, with as much speed as I could: so I took a man with me, and made a shot at a couple of Ducks, some six score paces off, and killed one, at which he wondered: so we returned forthwith, and dressed it, making more broth therewith, which he much desired; never did I see a man so low brought, recover in that measure in so short a time. The Fowl being extraordinary fat, I told *Hobbamock* I must take off the top thereof, saying it would make him very sick again if he did eat it; this he acquainted *Massassowat* therewith, who would not be persuaded to it, though I pressed it very much, shewing the strength thereof, and the weakness of his stomach, which could not possibly bear it. Notwithstanding he made a gross meal of it, and ate as much as would well have satisfied a man in health. About [31] an hour after he began to be very sick, and straining very much, cast up the broth again, and in over-straining himself, began to bleed at the nose, and so continued the space of four hours; then they all wished he had been ruled, concluding now he would die, which we much feared also. They asked me what I thought of him; I answered, his case was desperate, yet it might be it would save his life: for if it ceased in time, he would forthwith sleep and take rest, which was the principal thing he wanted. Not long after his blood stayed, and he slept at least six or eight hours; when he awaked I washed his face, and bathed and suppled[74] his beard and nose with a linen cloth: but on a sudden he chopped his nose in the water, and drew up

---

73. Smells.
74. Make soft.

some therein, and sent it forth again with such violence, as he began to
bleed afresh, then they thought there was no hope, but we perceived it
was but the tenderness of his nostril, and therefore told them I thought
it would stay presently, as indeed it did. [Figure 6]

The messengers were now returned, but finding his stomach come
to him, he would not have the chickens killed, but kept them for breed.
Neither durst we give him any physic which was then sent, because his
body was so much altered since our instructions, neither saw we any need,
not doubting now of his recovery, if he were careful. Many whilst we were
there came to see him, some by their report from a place not less than an
hundred miles. To all that came one of his chief men related the manner
of his sickness, how near he was spent, how amongst others his friends
the *English* came to see him, and how suddenly they recovered him to this
strength they saw, he being now able to sit upright of himself.

The day before our coming, another *Sachim* being there, told him, that
now he might see how hollow-hearted the *English* were, saying if we had
been such friends in deed, as we were in shew, we would have visited
him in this his sickness, using many arguments to withdraw his affections, and to persuade him to give way to some things against us, which
were motioned to him not long before: but upon [32] this his recovery,
he broke forth into these speeches; Now I see the *English* are my friends
and love me, and whilst I live I will never forget this kindness they have
shewed me. Whilst we were there, our entertainment exceeded all other
strangers. Diverse other things were worthy the noting, but I fear I have
been too tedious.

At our coming away, he called *Hobbamock* to him, & privately (none
hearing save two or three other of his *Pnieses*, who are of his Council)
revealed the plot of the *Massacheuseucks* before spoken of, against Master
Westons Colony, and so against us, saying that the people of *Nauset*,
Paomet, Succonet[75] *Mattachiest, Manomet Agowaywam,*[76] and the Ile of
Capawack[77] were joined with them; himself also in his sickness was earnestly solicited, but he would neither join therein, nor give way to any
of his. Therefore as we respected the lives of our Countrymen, and our
own after-safety, he advised us to kill the men of *Massachuset*, who were

---

75. Now Falmouth, Mass. See Young, *Chronicles of the Pilgrim Fathers*, 323, n. 2.
76. Young identifies this place as Agawam, now part of Wareham, Mass. See ibid., n. 3.
77. Martha's Vineyard, Mass. See ibid., n. 4.

The South part of Nevv-England, as it is Planted this yeare, 1634.

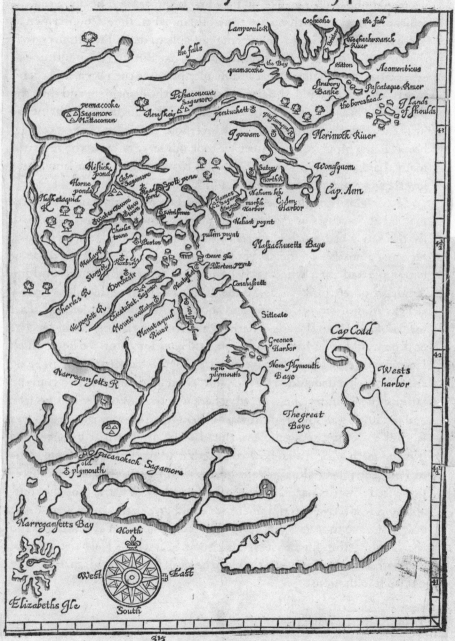

Figure 6. William Wood, *The South part of New-England, as it is Planted this yeare, 1634* (1635). Courtesy of the John Carter Brown Library at Brown University.

the authors of this intended mischief. And whereas we were wont to say, we would not strike a stroke till they first begun; if said he upon this intelligence, they make that answer, tell them, when their Countrymen at *Wichaguscusset* are killed, they being not able to defend themselves, that then it will be too late to recover their lives, nay through the multitude of adversaries they shall with great difficulty preserve their own, and therefore he counseled without delay to take away the principals, and then the plot would cease. With this he charged him thoroughly to acquaint me by the way, that I might inform the Governour thereof at my first coming home. Being fitted for our return, we took our leave of him, who returned many thanks to our Governour, and also to our selves for our labour and love: the like did all that were about him. So we departed.

That night through the earnest request of *Conbatant*, who til now remained at *Sawaams* or *Puckanokick*, we lodged with him at *Mattapuyst*. By the way I had much conference with him; so likewise at his house, he being a notable politician, yet full of merry jests & squibs,[78] & never better pleased than when [33] the like are returned again upon him. Amongst other things he asked me, If in case he were thus dangerously sick, as *Massassowat* had been, and should send word thereof to *Patuxet* for *Maskiet*, that is, Physic, whether then Mr Governour would send it? & if he would, whether I would come therewith to him? To both which I answered yea, whereat he gave me many joyful thanks. After that, being at his house he demanded further, how we durst being but two come so far into the Country? I answered, where was true love there was no fear, and my heart was so upright towards them that for mine own part I was fearless to come amongst them. But, said he, if your love be such, and it bring forth such fruits, how commeth it to pass, that when we come to *Patuxet*, you stand upon your guard, with the mouths of your Pieces presented towards us? Whereunto I answered, it was the most honourable and respective entertainment we could give them; it being an order amongst us so to receive our best respected friends: and as it was used on the Land, so the ships observed it also at Sea, which *Hobbamock* knew, and had seen observed. But shaking the head he answered, that he liked not such salutations.

---

78. A sarcastic comment.

Further, observing us to crave a blessing on our meat before we did eat, and after to give thanks for the same, he asked us what was the meaning of that ordinary custom? Hereupon I took occasion to tell them of Gods works of Creation, and Preservation, of his Laws and Ordinances, especially of the ten Commandments, all which they hearkened unto with great attention, and liked well of: only the seventh Commandment they excepted against, thinking there were many inconveniences in it, that a man should be tied to one woman: about which we reasoned a good time. Also I told them that whatsoever good things we had, we received from God, as the Author and giver thereof, and therefore craved his blessing upon that we had, and were about to eat, that it might nourish and strengthen our bodies, and having eaten sufficient, [34] being satisfied therewith, we again returned thanks to the same our God for that our refreshing, &c. This all of them concluded to be very well, and said, they believed almost all the same things, and that the same power that we called God, they called *Kietitan*. Much profitable conference was occasioned hereby, which would be too tedious to relate, yet was no less delightful to them, than comfortable[79] to us. Here we remained only that night, but never had better entertainment amongst any of them.

The day following, in our journey, *Hobbamock* told me of the private conference he had with *Massassowat,* and how he charged him perfectly to acquaint me therewith (as I shewed before) which having done, he used many arguments himself to move us thereunto; That night we lodged at *Namasket,* and the day following about the mid way between it and home, we met two *Indians,* who told us that Captain *Standish* was that day gone to the *Massachusets:* but contrary winds again drive him back, so that we found him at home; where the *Indian of Paomet* still was, being very importunate that the Captain should take the first opportunity of a fair wind to go with him, but their secret and villainous purposes being through Gods mercy now made known, the Governour caused Captain *Standish* to send him away without any distaste or manifestation of anger, that we might the better effect and bring to pass that which should be thought most necessary.

---

79. Here Winslow is likely using this word to mean: "Strengthening or supporting (morally or spiritually); encouraging, inspiriting, reassuring, cheering." See *Oxford English Dictionary,* 1st ed., s.v. "Comfortable," adj. 1a.

Before this journey we heard many complaints both by the *Indians* and some others of best desert amongst Master *Westons* Colony, how exceedingly their Company abased themselves by undirect means, to get victuals from the *Indians*, who dwelt not far from them, fetching them wood and water, &c. and all for a meals meat, whereas in the mean time, they might with diligence have gotten enough to have served them three or four times. Other by night broke the earth, and robbed the *Indians* store,[80] [35] for which they had been publicly stocked and whipped, and yet was there small amendment. This was about the end of February, at which time they had spent all their bread and corn, not leaving any for seed, neither would the *Indians* lend or sell them any more upon any terms. Hereupon they had thoughts to take it by violence, and to that spiked up every entrance into their Town (being well impaled) save one, with a full resolution to proceed. But some more honestly minded, advised *John Sanders* their Over-seer first to write to *Plimoth*, and if the Governour advised him thereunto, he might the better do it. This course was well liked, and an *Indian* was sent with all speed with a letter to our Governour, the contents whereof were to this effect; That being in great want, and their people daily falling down, he intended to go to *Munhiggen*, where was a Plantation of Sir *Ferdi: Gorges*, to buy bread from the Ships that came thither a fishing, with the first opportunity of wind; but knew not how the Colony would be preserved till his return: he had used all means both to buy and borrow of *Indians* whom he knew to be stored, and he thought maliciously with held it, and therefore was resolved to take it by violence, and only waited the return of the Messenger, which he desired should be hastened, craving his advice therein, promising also to make restitution afterward. The Governour upon the receipt hereof, asked the Messenger what store of corn they had, as if he had intended to buy of them; who answered very little more than that they reserved for seed, having already spared all they could. Forth-with the Governour and his Assistant sent for many of us to advise with them herein, who after serious consideration, no way approving of this intended course, the Governour answered his Letter, and caused many of us to set our hands thereto, the contents

---

80. Like the Plimoth colonists' decision to help themselves to food stores upon which they stumbled, the Wessagusset colonists' theft of the Massachusetts' food is mentioned several times in early texts about New England colonization. See the texts in section 3.

whereof were to this purpose; We altogether disliked their intendment, as being against the law of God and Nature, shewing how it would cross the worthy ends and proceedings of the Kings Majesty, and [36] his honourable Council for this place, both in respect of the peaceable enlarging of his Majesties Dominions, and also of the propagation of the knowledge and Law of God, and the glad tidings of salvation, which we and they were bound to seek, and were not to use such means as would breed a distaste in the Savages against our persons and professions, assuring them their Master would incur much blame hereby, neither could they answer the same; For our own parts our case was almost the same with theirs, having but a small quantity of Corn left, and were enforced to live on ground nuts, clams, mussels, and such other things as naturally the Country afforded, and which did and would maintain strength, and were easy to be gotten, all which things they had in great abundance, yea, Oysters also which we wanted, and therefore necessity could not be said to constrain them thereunto. Moreover, that they should consider, if they proceeded therein, all they could so get would maintain them but a small time, and then they must perforce seek their food abroad, which having made the *Indians* their enemies, would be very difficult for them, and therefore much better to begin a little the sooner, and so continue their peace, upon which course they might with good conscience desire and expect the blessing of God, whereas on the contrary they could not.

Also that they should consider their own weakness, being most swelled, and diseased in their bodies, and therefore the more unlikely to make their party good against them, and that they should not expect help from us in that or any the like unlawful actions. Lastly, that howsoever some of them might escape, yet the principal Agents should expect no better than the Galhouse,[81] whensoever any special Officer should be sent over by his Majesty, or his Council for *New England*, which we expected, and who would undoubtedly call them to account for the same. These were the contents of our Answer, which was directed to their whole Colony. Another particular [37] Letter our Governour sent to *John Sanders*, shewing how dangerous it would be for him above all others, being he was their leader and commander; and therefore in friendly manner advised him to desist.

---

81. Gallows.

With these Letters we dispatched the Messenger; Upon the receipt whereof they altered their determination, resolving to shift as they could, till the return of *John Sanders* from *Munhiggen*, who first coming to *Plimoth*, notwithstanding our own necessities, the Governour spared him some Corn to carry them to *Munhiggen*. But not having sufficient for the Ships store, he took a Shallop and leaving others with instructions to over-see things till his return, set forward about the end of February, so that he knew not of this conspiracy of the *Indians* before his going; neither was it known to any of us till our return from *Sawaams* or *Pucka-nokick*: At which time also another *Sachim* called *Wassapinewat*, brother to *Obtakiest* the *Sachim* of the *Massachusets*, who had formerly smarted for partaking with *Conbatant*, and fearing the like again, to purge himself revealed the same thing.

The three and twentieth of March being now come, which is a yearly Court day, the Governour having a double testimony, and many circumstances agreeing with the truth thereof, not being[82] to undertake war without the consent of the body of the Company; made known the same in public Court, offering it to the consideration of the Company, it being high time to come to resolution, how sudden soever it seemed to them, fearing it would be put in execution before we could give any intelligence thereof. This business was no less troublesome than grievous, and the more, because it is so ordinary in these times for men to measure things by the events thereof: but especially for that we knew no means to deliver our Countrymen and preserve our selves, than by returning their malicious and cruel purposes upon their own heads, and causing them to fall into the same pit [38] they had digged for others, though it much grieved us to shed the blood of those whose good we ever intended and aimed at, as a principal in all our proceedings. But in the end we came to this public conclusion, that because it was a matter of such weight as every man was not of sufficiency to judge, nor fitness to know because of many other *Indians* which daily as occasion serveth converse with us; therefore the Governour, his Assistant, and the Captain, should take such to themselves as they thought most meet, and conclude thereof; which done we came to this conclusion, That Captain *Standish* should take so

---

82. A word seems to have been omitted here.

many men as he thought sufficient to make his party good against all the
Indians in the *Massachuset-bay*; and because (as all men know that have
had to do in that kind) it is impossible to deal with them upon open
defiance, but to take them in such traps as they lay for others; therefore
he should pretend trade as at other times: but first go to the *English* and
acquaint them with the plot, and the end of his own coming, that comparing it with their carriages towards them he might the better judge of
the certainty of it, and more fitly take opportunity to revenge the same:
but should forbear if it were possible till such time as he could make sure
Wituwamat, that bloody and bold villain before spoken of, whose head
he had order to bring with him, that he might be a warning and terrour
to all of that disposition. Upon this Captain *Standish* made choice of
eight men, and would not take more because he would prevent jealousy,
knowing their guilty consciences would soon be provoked thereunto: but
on the next day before he could go, came one of Mr. *Westons* Company[83]
by land unto us, with his pack at his back, who made a pitiful narration
of their lamentable and weak estate, and of the *Indians* carriages, whose
boldness increased abundantly, insomuch as the victuals they got they
would take it out of their pots and eat before their faces, yea if any thing
they gain-said them, they were ready to hold a knife at their breasts; that
to give [39] them content, since *John Sanders* went to *Munhiggen*, they had
hanged one of them that stole their corn, and yet they regarded it not;
that another of their Company was turned Savage, that their people had
most forsaken the town, and made their rendezvous where they got their
victuals, because they would not take pains to bring it home; that they
had sold their clothes for corn, and were ready to starve both with cold
and hunger also, because they could not endure to get victuals by reason
of their nakedness; and that they were dispersed into three Companies
scarce having any powder and shot left. What would be the event of these
things (he said) he much feared; and therefore not daring to stay any
longer among them, though he knew not the way yet adventured to come
to us, partly to make known their weak and dangerous estate, as he conceived, and partly to desire he might there remain till things were better
settled at the other plantation. As this relation was grievous to us, so it

83. This man is Phenehas Pratt. See excerpts of his account in sections 1 and 3 below.

gave us good encouragement to proceed in our intendments, for which Captain *Standish* was now fitted, and the wind coming fair, the next day set forth for the *Massachusets*.

The *Indians* at the *Massachusets* missed this man, and suspecting his coming, to us as we conceive, sent one after him and gave out there that he would never come to *Patuxet*, but that some Wolves or Bears would eat him: but we know both by our own experience and the report of others, that though they find a man sleeping, yet so soon as there is life discerned they fear and shun him. This *Indian* missed him but very little, and missing him passed by the town and went to *Manomet*, whom we hoped to take at his return, as afterward we did. Now was our Fort made fit for service and some Ordnance mounted; and though it may seem long work it being ten months since it begun, yet we must note, that where so great a work is begun with such small means, a little time cannot bring to perfection: beside those works which [40] tend to the preservation of man, the enemy of mankind will hinder what in him lieth, sometimes blinding the judgment and causing reasonable men to reason against their own safety, as amongst us diverse seeing the work prove tedious, would have dissuaded from proceeding, flattering themselves with peace and security, and accounting it rather a work of superfluity and vain-glory, than simple necessity. But God (whose providence hath waked and as I may say, watched for us whilst we slept) having determined to preserve us from these intended treacheries, undoubtedly ordained this as a special means to advantage us and discourage our adversaries, and therefore so stirred up the hearts of the Governours and other forward instruments, as the work was just made serviceable against this needful and dangerous time, though we ignorant of the same. But that I may proceed, the *Indian* last mentioned in his return from *Manomet*, came through the town pretending still friendship and in love to see us, but as formerly others, so his end was to see whether we continued still in health and strength, or fell into weakness like their neighbors, which they hoped and looked for (though God in mercy provided better for us) and he knew would be glad tidings to his Country men. But here the Governour stayed him, and sending for him to the Fort, there gave the Guard charge of him as their prisoner, where he told him he must be contented to remain till the return of Captain *Standish* from the *Massachusets*, so he was locked in a chain to a staple in the Court of guard, and there kept. Thus was our Fort hanselled,[84] this being the first day as I take it, that ever any watch was there kept.

The Captain being now come to the *Massachusets*, went first to the ship,[85] but found neither man, or so much as a dog therein: upon the discharge of a Musket the Master and some others of the plantation shewed themselves, who were on the shore gathering ground-nuts, and getting other food. After salutation Captain *Standish* [41] asked them how they durst so leave the ship and live in such security, who answered like men senseless of their own misery, they feared not the *Indians*, but lived and suffered them to lodge with them, not having sword, or gun, or needing the same. To which the Captain answered, if there were no cause he was the gladder, but upon further inquiry, understanding that those in whom *John Sanders* had received most special confidence and left in his stead to govern the rest were at the Plantation, thither he went, and to be brief, made known the *Indians* purpose and the end of his own coming, as also (which formerly I omitted) that if afterward they durst not there stay, it was the intendment of the Governours and people of *Plimoth* there to receive them till they could be better provided: but if they conceived of any other course that might be more likely for their good, that himself should further them therein to the uttermost of his power. These men comparing other circumstances with that they now heard, answered, they could expect no better, and it was Gods mercy that they were not killed before his coming, desiring therefore that he would neglect no opportunity to proceed: Hereupon he advised them to secrecy, yet withal to send special command to one third of their Company that were farthest off to come home, and there enjoin them on pain of death to keep the town, himself allowing them a pint of *Indian* corn to a man for a day (though that store he had was spared out of our seed.) The weather proving very wet and stormy, it was the longer before he could do any thing.

In the mean time an *Indian* came to him and brought some furs, but rather to gather what he could from the Captains, than coming then for trade; and though the Captain carried things as smoothly as possibly he could, yet at his return he reported he saw by his eyes that he was angry

---

84. Used for the first time.
85. That is, the ship that brought the men to Wessagusset, probably the *Swan*.

in his heart, and therefore began to suspect themselves discovered. This caused one *Pecksuot* who was a *Pniese*, being a man of notable spirit to come to [42] *Hobbamock* who was then with them, and told him he understood that the Captain was come to kill himself and the rest of the Savages there, tell him said he we know it, but fear him not, neither will we shun him; but let him begin when he dare, he shall not take us at unawares: many times after diverse of them severally, or few together, came to the Plantation to him, where they would whet and sharpen the points of their knives before his face, and use many other insulting gestures and speeches. Amongst the rest, *Wituwamat* bragged of the excellency of his knife; on the end of the handle there was pictured a womans face, but said he, I have another at home wherewith I have killed both *French* and *English*, and that hath a mans face on it, and by and by these two must marry: Further he said of that knife he there had; *Hinnaim namen, hinnaim michen, matta cuts*: that is to say, By and by it should see, and by and by it should eat, but not speak. Also *Pecksuot* being a man of greater stature than the Captain, told him though he were a great Captain, yet he was but a little man: and said he, though I be no Sachim, yet I am a man of great strength and courage. These things the Captain observed, yet bare with patience for the present. On the next day, seeing he could not get many of them together at once, and this *Pecksuot* and *Wituwamat* both together, with another man, and a youth of some eighteen years of age, which was brother to *Wituwamat*, and villain-like trod in his steps, daily putting many tricks upon the weaker sort of men, and having about as many of his own Company in a room with them, gave the word to his men, and the door being fast shut began himself with *Pecksuot*, and snatching his own knife from his neck though with much struggling killed him therewith, the point whereof he had made as sharp as a needle, and ground the back also to an edge: *Wituwamat* and the other man, the rest killed, and took the youth, whom the Cap. caused to be hanged; but it is incredible how many [43] wounds these two Pnieses received before they died, not making any fearful noise, but catching at their weapons and striving to the last. *Hobbamock* stood by all this time as a spectator and meddled not, observing how our men demeaned themselves in this action; all being here ended, smiling he broke forth into these speeches to the Captain, Yester-day *Pecksuot* bragging of his own strength and stature, said, though you were a great Captain yet you were but a little man; but to day I see you are big enough to lay him on the ground. But to proceed, there being some women[86] at the same time, Captain *Standish* left them in the custody of Mr. *Westons* people at the town, and sent word to another Company that had intelligence of things to kill those *Indian* men that were amongst them, these killed two more: himself also with some of his own men went to another place, where they killed another, and through the negligence of one man an *Indian* escaped, who discovered and crossed[87] their proceedings.

Not long before this execution, three of Mr. *Westons* men which more regarded their bellies than any command or Commander, having formerly fared well with the *Indians* for making them Canoes, went again to the *Sachim* to offer their service, and had entertainment. The first night they came thither within night late came a Messenger with all speed, and delivered a sad and short message: Whereupon all the men gathered together, put on their boots and breeches, trusled[88] up themselves, and took their bows and arrows and went forth, telling them they went a hunting, and that at their return they should have venison enough. Being now gone, one being more ancient and wise than the rest, calling former things to mind, especially the Captains presence, and the straight charge that on pain of death none should go a Musket-shot from the plantation, and comparing this sudden departure of theirs there with, began to dislike and wish himself at home again, which was further off than diverse other dwelt: Hereupon he moved his fellows to [44] return but could not persuade them: so there being none but women left and the other that was turned savage, about midnight came away, forsaking the paths lest he should be pursued, and by this means saved his life.

Captain *Standish* took the one half of his men, and one or two of Mr. *Westons*, and *Hobbamock*, still seeking to make spoil of them and theirs. At length they espied a file of *Indians* which made towards them amain,[89] and there being a small advantage in the ground by reason of a hill near them, both Companies strove for it, Captain *Standish* got it, whereupon

---

86. Massachusett women.
87. Thwarted or opposed.
88. Winslow probably means "trussed" here, as in, to pack up belongings.
89. Violently, and with all one's force.

they retreated and took each man his tree, letting fly their arrows amain, especially at himself and *Hobbamock*, whereupon *Hobbamock* cast off his coat, and being a known Pniese, (theirs being now killed) chased them so fast as our people were not able to hold way with him, insomuch as our men could have but one certain mark and then but the arm and half face of a notable villain as he drew at Captain *Standish*, who together with another both discharged at once at him, and broke his arm; whereupon they fled into a swamp, when they were in the thicket they parleyed, but to small purpose, getting nothing but foul language. So our Captain dared the Sachim to come out and fight like a man, shewing how base and woman-like he was in tonguing[90] it as he did: but he refused and fled. So the captain returned to the Plantation, where he released the women and would not take their beaver coats from them, nor suffer the least discourtesy to be offered them. Now were Mr. *Westons* people resolved to leave their Plantation and go for *Munhiggen*, hoping to get passage and return with the fishing ships. The Captain told them, that for his own part he durst there live with fewer men than they were, yet since they were otherways minded, according to his order from the Governours and people of *Plimoth* he would help them with corn competent for their provision [45] by the way, which he did, scarce leaving himself more than brought them home. Some of them disliked the choice of the body to go to *Munhiggen*, and therefore desiring to go with him to *Plimoth*, he took them into the shallop: and seeing them set sail and clear of the *Massachuset bay*, he took leave and returned to *Plimoth*, whither he came in safety (blessed be God) and brought the head of *Wituwamat* with him.

Amongst the rest there was an *Indian* youth that was ever of a courteous and loving disposition towards us, he notwithstanding the death of his Countrymen came to the Captain without fear, saying his good conscience and love towards us emboldened him so to do. This youth confessed that the *Indians* intended to kill Mr. *Westons* people, and not to delay any longer than till they had two more Canoes or Boats, which Mr. *Westons* men would have finished by this time (having made them three already) had not the Captain prevented them, and the end of stay for those Boats, was to take their Ship therewith.

---

90. To assail with words. See *Oxford English Dictionary*, 1st ed., s.v. "Tongue," v., 1.

Now was the Captain returned and received with joy, the head being brought to the fort and there set up, the Governours and Captains with diverse others went up the same further, to examine the prisoner, who looked piteously on the head, being asked whether he knew it, he answered, yea: Then he confessed the plot, and that all the people provoked *Obtakiest* their *Sachim* thereunto, being drawn to it by their importunity: Five there were (he said) that prosecuted it with more eagerness than the rest, the two principal were killed, being *Pecksuot* and *Wituwamat*, whose head was there, the other three were *Powahs*, being yet living, and known unto us, though one of them was wounded, as aforesaid. For himself he would not acknowledge that he had any hand therein, begging earnestly for his life, saying, he was not a *Massachuset* man, but as a stranger lived with them. *Hobbamock* also gave a good report of him, and besought for him, but was bribed so [46] to do: Nevertheless, that we might shew mercy as well as extremity, the Governour released him, and the rather because we desired he might carry a message to *Obtakiest* his Master. No sooner were the irons from his legs, but he would have been gone, but the Governour bid him stay and fear not, for he should receive no hurt, and by *Hobbamock* commanded him to deliver this message to his Master; That for our parts, it never entered into our hearts to take such a course with them, till their own treachery enforced us thereunto, and therefore might thank themselves for their own over-throw, yet since he had begun, if again by any the like courses he did provoke him, his Country should not hold him, for he would never suffer him or his to rest in peace, till he had utterly consumed them, and therefore should take this as a warning. Further, that he should send to *Patuxet* the three Englishmen he had and not kill them; also that he should not spoil the pale and houses at *Wichaguscusset*, and that this Messenger should either bring the English, or an answer, or both, promising his safe return.

This message was delivered, and the party would have returned with answer, but was at first dissuaded by them, whom afterward they would but could not persuade to come to us. At length (though long) a Woman came and told us that *Obtakiest* was sorry that the English were killed before he heard from the Governour, otherwise he would have sent them. Also she said, he would fain make his peace again with us, but none of his men durst come to treat about it, having forsaken his dwelling, and daily removed from place to place, expecting when we would take further vengeance on him.

Concerning those other people that intended to join with the *Massachuseucks* against us, though we never went against any of them, yet this sudden and unexpected execution, together with the just judgment of God upon their guilty consciences, hath so terrified and amazed them, as in like manner they forsook their houses, running [47] to and fro like men distracted, living in swamps and other desert places, and so brought manifold diseases amongst themselves, whereof very many are dead, as *Canacum* the *Sachim* of *Manomet*, *Aspinet*, the *Sachim* of *Nauset*, and *Ianowh*,[91] *Sachim* of *Mattachuest*. This *Sachim* in his life, in the middest of these distractions, said the God of the English was offended with them, and would destroy them in his anger, and certainly it is strange to hear how many of late have, and still daily die amongst them, neither is there any likelihood it will easily cease, because through fear they set little or no Corn, which is the staff of life, and without which they cannot long preserve health and strength. From one of these places a boat was sent with presents to the Governour, hoping thereby to work their peace, but the boat was cast away, and three of the persons drowned, not far from our plantation, only one escaped, who durst not come to us, but returned, so as none of them dare come amongst us.

I fear I have been too tedious both in this and other things, yet when I considered how necessary a thing it is that the truth and grounds of this action, especially should be made known, and the several dispositions of that dissolved Colony, whose reports undoubtedly will be as various, I could not but enlarge my self where I thought to be most brief; neither durst I be too brief, least I should eclipse and rob God of that honour, glory, and praise, which belongeth to him for preserving us from falling when we were at the pits brim, and yet feared nor knew not that we were in danger.

The[92] month of April being now come, on all hands we began to prepare for Corn. And because there was no Corn left before this time, save that was preserved for seed, being also hopeless of relief by supply, we thought best to leave off all other works, and prosecute that as most

---

91. Iyanough.
92. Winslow's margin note: *Anno* 1623.

necessary. And because there was no small hope of doing good in that common course of labour that formerly we were in, for that the Governours that followed men to their [48] labours, had nothing to give men for their necessities, and therefore could not so well exercise that command over them therein as formerly they had done, especially considering that self-love wherewith every man (in a measure more or less) loveth and preferreth his own good before his neighbors,[93] and also the base disposition of some drones,[94] that as at other times so now especially would be most burdenous to the rest; It was therefore thought best that every man should use the best diligence he could for his own preservation, both in respect of the time present, and to prepare his own Corn for the year following: and bring in a competent portion for the maintenance of public Officers, Fishermen, &c. which could not be freed from their calling without greater inconveniences. This course was to continue till harvest, and then the Governours to gather in the appointed portion, for the maintenance of themselves and such others as necessity constrained to exempt from this condition. Only if occasion served upon any special service they might employ such as they thought most fit to execute the same, during this appointed time, and at the end thereof all men to be employed by them in such service as they thought most necessary for the general good. And because there is great difference in the ground, that therefore a set quantity should be set down for a person, and each man to have his fall by lot, as being most just and equal, and against which no man could except.

At a general meeting of the Company, many courses were propounded, but this approved and followed, as being the most likely for the present and future good of the Company; and therefore before this month began to prepare our ground against seed-time. In the middest of April we began to set, the weather being then seasonable, which much encouraged us, giving us good hopes of after plenty: the setting season is good till the latter end of May. But it pleased God for our further chastisement, to send a great drowth, insomuch, as in six weeks after the [49] latter setting there scarce fell any rain, so that the stalk of that was first set began

---

93. Robert Cushman, one of the colonists' spiritual leaders, had preached a sermon about the dangerous of self-love in 1621 at Plimoth. See the selection from Cushman in section 2.

94. Those who are lazy.

to send forth the ear before it came to half growth, and that which was later, not like to yield any at all, both blade and stalk hanging the head, and changing the color in such manner, as we judged it utterly dead: our Beans also ran not up according to their wonted manner, but stood at a stay, many being parched away, as though they had been scorched before the fire. Now were our hopes overthrown, and we discouraged, our joy being turned into mourning.

To add also to this sorrowful estate in which we were, we heard of a supply that was sent unto us many months since, which having two repulses before, was a third time in company of another ship three hundred Leagues at Sea, and now in three months time heard no further of her, only the signs of a wreck were seen on the coast, which could not be judged to be any other than the same. So that at once God seemed to deprive us of all future hopes. The most courageous were now discouraged, because God which hitherto had been our only Shield and Supporter, now seemed in his anger to arm himself against us; and who can withstand the fierceness of his wrath.

These, and the like considerations moved not only every good man privately to enter into examination with his own estate between God and his conscience, and so to humiliation before him: but also more solemnly to humble our selves together before the Lord by fasting and prayer. To that end a day was appointed by public authority, and set a-part from all other employments, hoping that the same God which had stirred us up hereunto, would be moved hereby in mercy to look down upon us, & grant the request of our dejected souls, if our continuance there might any way stand with his glory and our good. But oh the mercy of our God! Who was as ready to hear as we to ask: For though in the morning when we assembled together, the heavens were as clear and the drought as like to continue as ever it was: yet (our exercise [50] continuing some eight or nine hours) before our departure the weather was over-cast, the clouds gathered together on all sides, and on the next morning distilled such soft, sweet, and moderate showers of rain, continuing some fourteen days, and mixed with such seasonable weather, as it was hard to say whether our withered Corn, or drooping affections were most quickened or revived. Such was the bounty and goodness of our God. Of this the *Indians* by means of *Hobbamock* took notice: who being then in the

Town, and this exercise in the midst of the week, said, it was but three days since Sunday, and therefore demanded of a boy what was the reason thereof? Which when he knew and saw what effects followed thereupon, he and all of them admired the goodness of our God towards us, that wrought so great a change in so short a time, shewing the difference between their conjuration, and our invocation on the name of God for rain; theirs being mixed with such storms and tempests, as sometimes in stead of doing them good, it layeth the Corn flat on the ground, to their prejudice: but ours in so gentle and seasonable a manner, as they never observed the like.

At the same time Captain *Standish* being formerly employed by the Governour to buy provisions for the refreshing of the Colony, returned with the same, accompanied with one Mr *David Tomson*, a Scotchman, who also that Spring began a Plantation twenty five leagues northeast from us, near *Smiths* Iles, at a place called *Pascatoquack*, where he liketh well.[95] Now also heard we of the third repulse that our supply had, of their safe though dangerous return into *England*, and of their preparation to come to us. So that having these many signs of Gods favour and acceptation, we thought it would be great ingratitude, if secretly we should smother up the same, or content our selves with private thanksgiving for that which by private prayer could not be obtained. And therefore another solemn day was set a-part and appointed for that end, [51] wherein we returned glory, honour, and praise, with all thankfulness to our good God, which dealt so graciously with us, whose name for these and all other his mercies towards his Church and chosen ones, by them be blessed and praised now and evermore, Amen.

In the latter end of July and the beginning of August, came two Ships with supply unto us, who brought all their passengers, except one, in health, who recovered in short time, who also notwithstanding, all our wants and hardship (blessed be God) found not any one sick person amongst us at the Plantation. The bigger Ship called the *Anne* was hired, and there again freighted back, from whence we set sail the tenth of September. The lesser called the little *James*, was built for the company at their charge. She was now also fitted for Trade and discovery to the

---

95. Tomson worked for Ferdinando Gorges; he settled temporarily near the Piscataqau River. See Young, *Chronicles of the Pilgrim Fathers*, 350–51, n. 1.

South-ward of Cape *Cod*, and almost ready to set sail, whom I pray God to bless in her good and lawful proceedings.

Thus have I made a true and full Narration of the state of our Plantation, and such things as were most remarkable therein since Decemb. 1621. If I have omitted any thing, it is either through weakness of memory, or because I judged it not material: I confess my style rude, and unskillfulness in the task I undertook, being urged thereunto by opportunity, which I knew to be wanting in others, and but for which I would not have undertaken the same; yet as it is rude so it is plain, and therefore the easier to be understood; wherein others may see that which we are bound to acknowledge, *viz.* That if ever any people in these later ages were upheld by the providence of God after a more special manner than others, then we: and therefore are the more bound to celebrate the memory of his goodness, with everlasting thankfulness. For in these forenamed straits, such was our state, as in the morning we had often our food to seek for the day, and yet performed the duties of our Callings, I mean other daily labours, to provide for after time: and though at some [52] times in some seasons at noon I have seen men stagger by reason of faintness for want of food, yet ere night by the good providence and blessing of God, we have enjoyed such plenty as though the windows of heaven had been opened unto us. How few, weak, and raw were we at our first beginning, and there settling, and in the middest of barbarous enemies? yet God wrought our peace for us. How often have we been at the pits brim, and in danger to be swallowed up, yea, not knowing, till afterward that we were in peril? and yet God preserved us: yea, and from how many that we yet know not of, he that knoweth all things can best tell: So that when I seriously consider of things, I cannot but think that God hath a purpose to give that Land as an inheritance to our Nation, and great pity it were that it should long lie in so desolate a state, considering it agreeth so well with the constitution of our bodies, being both fertile, and so temperate for heat and cold, as in that respect one can scarce distinguish *New-England* from *Old*.

A few things I thought meet to add hereunto, which I have observed amongst the *Indians*, both touching their Religion, and sundry other Customs amongst them. And first, whereas my self and others, in former Letters (which came to the Press against my will and knowledge) wrote, that the *Indians* about us are a people without any Religion, or knowledge of any God, therein I erred, though we could then gather no better:[96] For as they conceive[97] of many divine powers, so of one whom they call *Kiehtan*, to be the principal and maker of all the rest, and to be made by none: He (they say) created the heavens, earth, sea, and all creatures contained therein. [Figure 7] Also that he made one man and one woman, of whom they and we and all mankind came: but how they became so far dispersed that know they not. At first they say, there was no *Sachim*, or *King*, but *Kiehtan*, who dwelleth above in the Heavens, whither all good men go when [53] they die, to see their friends, and have their fill of all things: This his habitation lieth far West-ward in the heavens, they say; thither the bad men go also, and knock at his door, but he bids them *Quatchet*, that is to say, Walk abroad, for there is no place for such; so that they wander in restless want and penury: Never man saw this *Kiehtan*; only old men tell them of him, and bid them tell their children, yea, to charge them to teach their posterities the same, and lay the like charge upon them. This power they acknowledge to be good, and when they would obtain any great matter, meet together, and cry unto him, and so likewise for plenty, victory, &c. sing, dance, feast, give thanks, and hang up Garlands and other things in memory of the same.

Another power they worship, whom they call *Hobbamock*, and to the Norward of us *Hobbamoqui*; this as far as we can conceive is the Devil, him they call upon to cure their wounds and diseases.[98] When they are curable, he persuades them he sends the same for some conceived anger against them, but upon their calling upon him can and doth help them: But when they are mortal, and not curable in nature, then he persuades them *Kiehtan* is angry and sends them, whom none can cure: in so much, as in that respect only they somewhat doubt whether he be simply good, and therefore in sickness never call upon him.

This *Hobbamock* appears in sundry forms unto them, as in the shape of a Man, a Deer, a Fawn, an Eagle, &c. but most ordinarily a Snake: He

---

96. Winslow initially claimed that the Natives had no religion in *A Relation Or Journal*. See section 3, "Letter Sent From *New-England*."

97. Winslow's margin note: The meaning of the word *Kiehtan*, I think hath reference to Antiquity, for *Chise* is an old man, and *Kiehchise*, a man that exceedeth in age.

98. Although this deity has the same name as the Wampanoag translator, there does not seem to be any relation between the two.

times in some seasons at noone I haue seene men stagger
by reason of faintnesse for want of foode, yet ere night
by the good providence and blessing of God, wee haue en-
ioyed such plentie as though the windowes of heauen had
beene opened vnto vs. How few, weake, and raw were we
at our first beginning, and there setling, and in the middest
of barbarous enemies? yet God wrought our peace for vs.
How often haue wee beene at the pits brim, and in danger
to be swallowed vp, yea, not knowing, till afterward that
we were in perill? and yet God preserved vs: yea, and from
how many that we yet know not of, he that knoweth all
things can best tell: So that when I seriously consider of
things, I cannot but thinke that God hath a purpose to
giue that Land as an inheritance to our Nation, and great
pittie it were that it should long lie in so desolate a state,
considering it agreeth so well with the constitution of our
bodies, being both fertile, and so temperate for heate and
cold, as in that respect one can scarce distinguish *New-
England* from *Old.*

  A few things I thought meet to adde hereunto, which
I haue obserued amongst the *Indians*, both touching their
Religion, and sundry other Customes amongst them.
And first, whereas my selfe and others, in former Letters (which came to the Presse against my will and knowledge) wrote, that the *Indians* about vs are a people without any Religion, or knowledge of any God, therein I erred, though we could then gather no better : For as they
conceiue of many divine powers, so of one whom they
call *Kiehtan*, to be the principall and maker of all the rest,
and to be made by none: He (they say) created the heavens, earth, sea, and all creatures contained therein. Also
that he made one man and one woman, of whom they and
wee and all mankinde came : but how they became so
farre dispersed that know they not. At first they say, there
was no *Sachim*, or *King*, but *Kiehtan*, who dwelleth a-
boue in the Heavens, whither all good men goe when
                                                        they

The meaning of the word, Kiehtan, I thinke hath reference to Antiquitie, for that Chise is an old man, and Kiehchise, a man that exceedeth in age.

Figure 7. Edward Winslow, *Good News,* page 52 with marginal note (1624). Courtesy of the John Carter Brown Library at Brown University.

appears not to all but the chiefest and most judicious amongst them, though all of them strive to attain to that hellish height of honour.

He appeareth most ordinary and is most conversant with three sorts of people, one I confess I neither know by name nor office directly: Of these they [54] have few but esteem highly of them, and think that no weapon can kill them: another they call by the name of *Powah*, and the third *Pniese*.

The office and duty of the *Powah* is to be exercised principally in calling upon the Devil, and curing diseases of the sick or wounded. The common people join with him in the exercise of invocation, but do only assent, or as we term it, say *Amen* to that he saith, yet sometime break out into a short musical note with him. The *Powah* is eager and free in speech, fierce in countenance, and joineth many antic[99] and labourious gestures with the same over the party diseased. If the party be wounded he will also seem to suck the wound, but if they be curable (as they say) he toucheth it not, but a Skooke, that is the Snake, or Wobsacuck, that is the Eagle, sitteth on his shoulder and licks the same. This none see but the *Powah*, who tells them he doth it himself. If the party be otherwise diseased, it is accounted sufficient if in any shape he but come into the house, taking it for an undoubted sign of recovery.

And as in former ages *Apollo* had his temple at *Delphos*, and *Diana* at *Ephesus*;[100] so have I heard them call upon some as if they had their residence in some certain places, or because they appeared in those forms in the same. In the *Powahs* speech he promiseth to sacrifice many skins of beasts, kettles, hatchets, beads, knives, and other the best things they have to the fiend, if he will come to help the party diseased: But whether they perform it I know not. The other practises I have seen, being necessarily called at some times to be with their sick, and have used the best arguments I could make them understand against the same: They have told me I should see the Devil at those times come to the party, but I assured my self and them of the contrary, which so proved: yea, themselves have confessed they never saw him when any of us were present. In desperate and extraordinary hard travail in child-birth, when the party cannot be

---

99. Grotesque or bizarre.

100. Apollo was the Greek god of poetry and of medicine; his twin, Diana, the goddess of hunting, as well as of childbirth. Winslow is referring here to classical Greek sites of temples for these gods.

delivered by the [55] ordinary means, they send for this *Powah*, though ordinarily their travail is not so extreme as in our parts of the world, they being of a more hardy nature; for on the third day after child-birth I have seen the mother with the infant upon a small occasion in cold weather in a boat upon the Sea.

Many sacrifices the *Indians* use, and in some cases kill children.[101] It seemeth they are various in their religious worship in a little distance, and grow more and more cold in their worship to *Kiehtan;* saying in their memory he was much more called upon. The *Nanohiggansets* exceed in their blind devotion, and have a great spacious house wherein only some few (that are as we may term them Priests) come: thither at certain known times resort all their people, and offer almost all the riches they have to their gods, as kettles, skins, hatchets, beads, knives, &c. all which are cast by the Priests into a great fire that they make in the midst of the house, and there consumed to ashes. To this offering every man bringeth freely, and the more he is known to bring, hath the better esteem of all men. This the other *Indians* about us approve of as good, and wish their *Sachims* would appoint the like: and because the plague hath not reigned at *Nanohigganset* as at other places about them, they attribute to this custom there used.

The *Pnieses* are men of great courage and wisdom, and to these also the Devil appeareth more familiarly than to others, and as we conceive maketh covenant with them to preserve them from death, by wounds, with arrows, knives, hatchets, &c. or at least both themselves and especially the people think themselves to be freed from the same. And though against their battles all of them by painting disfigure themselves, yet they are known by their courage and boldness, by reason whereof one of them will chase almost an hundred men, for they account it death for whomsoever stand in their way. These are highly esteemed of all sorts of people, and are of the *Sachims* [56] Council, without whom they will not war or undertake any weighty business. In war their *Sachims* for their more safety go in the midst of them. They are commonly men of the greatest stature & strength, and such as will endure most hardness, and yet are more dis-

---

101. No evidence exists that New England Algonquians killed children as part of their ceremonies. Winslow probably observed ceremonies in which Algonquians burned some of their goods as a sacrifice. See Kupperman, *Indians and English*, 113–14.

creet, courteous, and humane in their carriages than any amongst them, scorning theft, lying, and the like base dealings, and stand as much upon their reputation as any men.

And to the end they may have store of these, they train up the most forward and likeliest boys from their childhood in great hardness, and make them abstain from dainty meat, observing diverse orders prescribed, to the end that when they are of age the Devil may appear to them, causing to drink the juice of Sentry[102] and other bitter herbs till they cast, which they must disgorge into the platter, and drink again, and again, till at length through extraordinary oppressing of nature it will seem to be all blood, and this the boys will do with eagerness at the first, and so continue till by reason of faintness they can scarce stand on their legs, and then must go forth into the cold: also they beat their shins with sticks, and cause them to run through bushes, stumps, and brambles, to make them hardy and acceptable to the Devil, that in time he may appear unto them.[103]

Their *Sachims* cannot be all called Kings, but only some few of them, to whom the rest resort for protection, and pay homage unto them, neither may they war with-out their knowledge and approbation, yet to be commanded by the greater as occasion serveth. Of this sort is *Massassowat* our friend, and *Conanacus* of *Nanohiggenset* our supposed enemy.

Every *Sachim* taketh care for the widow and fatherless, also for such as are aged, and any way maimed, if their friends be dead or not able to provide for them.

A *Sachim* will not take any to wife but such an one as is equal to him in birth, otherwise they say their seed would in time become ignoble, and though they have [57] many other wives, yet are they no other than concubines or servants, and yield a kind of obedience to the principal, who ordereth the family, and them in it. The like their men observe also, and will adhere to the first during their lives; but put away the other at their pleasure.

This government is successive and not by choice. If the father die before the son or daughter be of age, then the child is committed to the

---

102. Centaury, a bitter herb.
103. In such initiation ceremonies, young men attempted to become sensitive to supernatural or non-human beings, not necessarily the devil.

protection and tuition of some one amongst them, who ruleth in his stead till he be of age, but when that is I know not.

Every *Sachim* knoweth how far the bounds and limits of his own Country extendeth, and that is his own proper inheritance, out of that if any of his men desire land to set their corn, he giveth them as much as they can use, and sets them their bounds. In this circuit whosoever hunteth, if they kill any venison, bring him his fee, which is the fore parts of the same, if it be killed on the land, but if in the water, then the skin thereof: The great *Sachims* or Kings, know their own bounds or limits of land, as well as the rest.

All travelers or strangers for the most part lodge at the *Sachims*, when they come they tell them how long they will stay, and to what place they go, during which time they receive entertainment according to their persons, but want not.

Once a year the *Pnieses* use to provoke the people to bestow much corn on the *Sachim*. To that end they appoint a certain time and place near the *Sachims* dwelling, where the people bring many baskets of corn, and make a great stack thereof. There the *Pnieses* stand ready to give thanks to the people on the *Sachims* behalf, and after acquainteth the *Sachim* therewith, who fetcheth the same, and is no less thankful, bestowing many gifts on them.

When any are visited with sickness, their friends resort unto them for their comfort, and continue with them oft- [58] times till their death or recovery. If they die they stay a certain time to mourn for them. Night and morning they perform this duty many days after the burial in a most doleful manner, insomuch as though it be ordinary and the note musical, which they take one from another, and all together, yet it will draw tears from their eyes, & almost from ours also. But if they recover then because their sickness was chargeable, they send corn and other gifts unto them at a certain appointed time, whereat they feast and dance, which they call *Commoco*.

When they bury the dead they sew up the corpse in a mat and so put it in the earth. If the party be a *Sachim* they cover him with many curious mats, and bury all his riches with him, and enclose the grave with a pale. If it be a child the father will also put his own most special jewels and ornaments in the earth with it, also will cut his hair and disfigure himself very much in token of sorrow. If it be the man or woman of the house, they will pull down the mats and leave the frame standing, and bury them in or near the same, and either remove their dwelling or give over house-keeping.

The men employ themselves wholly in hunting, and other exercises of the bow, except at some times they take some pains in fishing.

The women live a most slavish life, they carry all their burdens, set and dress their corn, gather it in, seek out for much of their food, beat and make ready the corn to eat, and have all household care lying upon them.

The younger sort reverence the elder, and do all mean offices whilst they are together, although they be strangers. Boys and girls may not wear their hair like men and women, but are distinguished thereby.

A man is not accounted a man till he do some notable act, or shew forth such courage and resolution as becometh his place. The men take much tobacco, but for boys so to do they account it odious.

All their names are significant and variable, for when [59] they come to the state of men and women, they alter them according to their deeds or dispositions.

When a maid is taken in marriage she first cutteth her hair, and after weareth a covering on her head till her hair be grown out. Their women are diversely disposed, some as modest as they will scarce talk one with another in the company of men, being very chaste also: yet other some light, lascivious and wanton.

If a woman have a bad husband, or cannot affect him, and there be war or opposition between that and any other people, she will run away from him to the contrary party and there live, where they never come unwelcome: for where are most women, there is greatest plenty.

When a woman hath her monthly terms she separateth her self from all other company, and liveth certain days in a house alone: after which she washeth her self and all that she hath touched or used, and is again received to her husbands bed or family.

For adultery the husband will beat his wife and put her away, if he please. Some common strumpets there are as well as in other places, but they are such as either never married, or widows, or put away for adultery: for no man will keep such an one to wife.

In matters of unjust and dis-honest dealing the *Sachim* examineth and punisheth the same. In case of thefts, for the first offence he is disgracefully rebuked, for the second beaten by the *Sachim* with a cudgel on the naked back, for the third he is beaten with many strokes, and hath his nose slit upward, that thereby all men may both know and shun him. If any man kill another, he must likewise die for the same. The *Sachim* not only passeth the sentence upon malefactors, but executeth the same with his own hands, if the party be then present; if not, sendeth his own knife in case of death, in the hands of others to perform the same. But if the offender be to receive other punishment, he will not receive the same but from the [60] *Sachim* himself, before whom being naked he kneeleth, and will not offer to run away though he beat him never so much, it being a greater disparagement for a man to cry during the time of his correction, than is his offence and punishment.

As for their apparel they wear breeches and stockings in one like some *Irish*, which is made of Deer skins, and have shoes of the same leather.[104] They wear also a Deers skin loose about them like a cloak, which they will turn to the weather side. In this habit they travel, but when they are at home or come to their journeys end, presently they pull off their breeches, stockings, and shoes, wring out the water if they be wet, and dry them, and rub or chafe the same. Though these be off, yet have they another small garment that covereth their secrets. The men wear also when they go abroad in cold weather an Otter or Fox skin on their right arm, but only their bracer on the left. Women and all of that sex wear strings about their legs, which the men never do.

The people are very ingenious and observative, they keep account of time by the moon, and winters or summers; they know diverse of the stars by name, in particular, they know the North-star and call it maske, which is to say the bear. Also they have many names for the winds. They will guess very well at the wind and weather before hand, by observations in the heavens. They report also, that some of them can cause the wind to blow in what part they list,[105] can raise storms and tempests which they

---

104. English colonists frequently compared Native Americans to the Irish, especially in the early years of colonization. In part, these comparisons resulted from the fact that many colonists served in military campaigns in Ireland before traveling to the New World (most famously Humphrey Gilbert and Ralph Lane). In addition, these comparisons arose because English people viewed the Irish as savage and employed their conceptions of civilization (and the lack thereof) to describe Native peoples. See Quinn, *Elizabethans and the Irish*, and Canny, "Ideology of English Colonization."

105. Desire.

usually do when they intend the death or destruction of other people, that by reason of the unseasonable weather they may take advantage of their enemies in their houses. At such times they perform their greatest exploits, and in such seasons when they are at enmity with any, they keep more careful watch than at other times.

As for the language it is very copious, large, and difficult, as yet we cannot attain to any great measure thereof; [61] but can understand them, and explain our selves to their understanding, by the help of those that daily converse with us. And though there be difference in an hundred miles distance of place, both in language and manners, yet not so much but that they very well understand each other. And thus much of their lives and manners.

Instead of Records and Chronicles, they take this course, where any remarkable act is done, in memory of it, either in the place, or by some path-way near adjoining, they make a round hole in the ground about a foot deep, and as much over, which when others passing by behold, they enquire the cause and occasion of the same, which being once known, they are careful to acquaint all men, as occasion serveth therewith. And lest such holes should be filled, or grown up by any accident, as men pass by they will oft renew the same: By which means many things of great Antiquity are fresh in memory. So that as a man travelleth, if he can understand his guide, his journey will be the less tedious, by reason of the many historical Discourses will be related unto him.

In all this it may be said, I have neither praised nor dispraised the Country: and since I lived so long therein, my judgment thereof will give no less satisfaction to them that know me, than the Relation of our proceedings. To which I answer, that as in one so of the other, I will speak as sparingly as I can, yet will make known what I conceive thereof.

And first for that Continent, on which we are called *New England*, although it hath ever been conceived by the English to be part of that main Land adjoining to *Virginia*, yet by relation of the *Indians* it should appear to be otherwise: for they affirm confidently, that it is an Island, and that either the *Dutch* or *French* pass through from Sea to Sea, between us and *Virginia*, and drive a great Trade in the same. The name of that inlet of the Sea they call *Mohegon*, which I take to be the same which we call *Hudsons*-River, up which Master *Hudson* went many [62] Leagues, and for want of means (as I hear) left it undiscovered. For confirmation of this, their opinion is thus much; Though *Virginia* be not above an hundred and fifty Leagues from us, yet they never heard of *Powhatan*,[106] or knew that any English were planted in his Country, save only by us and *Tisquantum*, who went in an English Ship thither: And therefore it is the more probable, because the water is not passable for them, who are very adventurous in their Boats.

Then for the temperature of the air, in almost three years experience, I can scarce distinguish *New-England* from *Old England*, in respect of heat, and cold, frost, snow, rain, winds, &c. Some object, because our Plantation lieth in the Latitude of 42. it must needs be much hotter.[107] I confess, I cannot give the reason of the contrary; only experience teacheth us, that if it do exceed *England*, it is so little as must require better judgments to discern it. And for the Winter, I rather think (if there be difference) it is both sharper and longer in *New England* than *Old*; and yet the want of those comforts in the one which I have enjoyed in the other, may deceive my judgment also. But in my best observation, comparing our own condition with the Relations of other parts of America, I cannot conceive of any to agree better with the constitution of the English, not being oppressed with extremity of heat, nor nipped with biting cold, by which means, blessed be God, we enjoy our health, notwithstanding, those difficulties we have under-gone, in such a measure as would have been admired, if we had lived in *England* with the like means.

The day is two hours longer than here when it is at the shortest, and as much shorter there, when it is at the longest.

The soil is variable, in some places mould,[108] in some clay, others, a mixed sand, &c. The chiefest grain is the *Indian* Mays, or *Ginny*-Wheat; the seed-time beginneth in midst of April, and continueth good till the midst of [63] May. Our harvest beginneth with September. This corn

---

106. Colonists referred to the werowance (the Virginian word for sachem) of the Powhatan people in Virginia by the same name as the tribe. Winslow here probably means to refer to Wahunsenacawh, the leader of the Powhatans when Jamestown was established. See Allen, *Pocahontas: Medicine Woman*, 21. On the Powhatans, see also Richter, "Tsenacommacah and the Atlantic World," and Rountree, *Powhatan Indians of Virginia*.

107. Winslow is referring to the belief that New England was warmer than England because the colony was located in a southern latitude compared to England. See Kupperman, "Fear of Hot Climates" and "Puzzle of the American Climate."

108. Loose soil, suitable for cultivation.

increaseth in great measure, but is inferiour in quantity to the same in *Virginia*, the reason I conceive, is because *Virginia* is far hotter than it is with us, it requiring great heat to ripen; but whereas it is objected against *New-England*, that Corn will not there grow, except the ground be manured with fish? I answer, That where men set with fish (as with us) it is more easy so to do than to clear ground and set without some five or six years, and so begin anew, as in *Virginia* and else-where. Not but that in some places, where they cannot be taken with ease in such abundance, the *Indians* set four years together without, and have as good Corn or better than we have that set with them, though indeed I think if we had Cattle to till the ground, it would be more profitable and better agreeable to the soil, to sow Wheat, Rye, Barley, Peas, and Oats, than to set Mays, which our *Indians* call *Ewachim*: for we have had experience that they like and thrive well; and the other will not be procured without good labour and diligence, especially at seed-time, when it must also be watched by night to keep the Wolves from the fish, till it be rotten, which will be in fourteen days; yet men agreeing together, and taking their turns it is not much.

Much might be spoken of the benefit that may come to such as shall here plant by Trade with the *Indians* for Furs, if men take a right course for obtaining the same, for I dare presume upon that small experience I have had, to affirm, that the *English*, *Dutch*, and *French*, return yearly many thousand pounds profits by Trade only from that *Island*, on which we are seated.

Tobacco may be there planted, but not with that profit as in some other places, neither were it profitable there to follow it, though the increase were equal, because fish is a better and richer Commodity, and more necessary, which may be and are there had in as great abundance as in any other part of the world; Witness the West-country [64] Merchants of *England*, which return incredible gains yearly from thence. And if they can so do which here buy their salt at a great charge, and transport more Company to make their voyage, than will sail their Ships, what may the planters expect when once they are seated, and make the most of their salt there, and employ themselves at least eight months in fishing, whereas the other fish but four, and have their ship lie dead in the harbour all the time, whereas such shipping as belong to plantations, may take freight

of passengers or cattle thither, and have their lading[109] provided against
they come. I confess, we have come so far short of the means to raise such
returns, as with great difficulty we have preserved our lives; insomuch, as
when I look back upon our condition, and weak means to preserve the
same, I rather admire at Gods mercy and providence in our preservation,
than that no greater things have been effected by us. But though our
beginning have been thus raw, small, and difficult, as thou hast seen, yet
the same God that hath hitherto led us through the former, I hope will
raise means to accomplish the latter. Not that we altogether, or principally
propound profit to be the main end of that we have undertaken, but the
glory of God, and the honour of our Country, in the enlarging of his
Majesties Dominions, yet wanting outward means, to set things in that
forwardness we desire, and to further the latter by the former, I thought
meet to offer both to consideration, hoping that where Religion and profit
jump together (which is rare) in so honourable an action, it will encourage
every honest man, either in person or purse, to set forward the same, or
at least-wise to commend the well-fare thereof in his daily prayers to the
blessing of the blessed God.

I will not again speak of the abundance of fowl, store of Venison, and
variety of Fish, in their seasons, which might encourage many to go in
their persons, only I advise all such before hand to consider, that as they
hear of Countries that abound with the good creatures of [65] God, so
means must be used for the taking of every one in his kind, and therefore
not only to content themselves that there is sufficient, but to foresee how
they shall be able to obtain the same, otherwise, as he that walketh *London* streets, though he be in the middest of plenty, yet if he want means, is
not the better but hath rather his sorrow increased by the sight of that he
wanteth, and cannot enjoy it: so also there, if thou want art and other nec-
essaries thereunto belonging, thou mayest see that thou wantest, and thy
heart desireth, and yet be never the better for the same. Therefore if thou
see thine own insufficiency of thy self, then join to some others, where
thou mayest in some measure enjoy the same, otherwise assure thy self,
thou art better where thou art. Some there be that thinking altogether

---

109. Cargo.

of their present wants they enjoy here, and not dreaming of any there, through indiscretion plunge themselves into a deeper sea of misery. As for example, it may be here, rent and firing are so chargeable, as without great difficulty a man cannot accomplish the same; never considering, that as he shall have no rent to pay, so he must build his house before he have it, and peradventure may with more ease pay for his fuel here, than cut and fetch it home, if he have not cattle to draw it there; though there is no scarcity but rather too great plenty.

I write not these things to dissuade any that shall seriously upon due examination set themselves to further the glory of God, and the honour of our Country, in so worthy an Enterprise, but rather to discourage such as with too great lightness undertake such courses, who peradventure strain themselves and their friends for their passage thither, and are no sooner there, than seeing their foolish imagination made void, are at their wits end, and would give ten times so much for their return, if they could procure it, and out of such discontented passions [66] and humors, spare not to lay that imputation upon the Country, and others, which themselves deserve.

As for example, I have heard some complain of others for their large reports of *New-England*, and yet because they must drink water and want many delicates they here enjoyed, could presently return with their mouths full of clamours. And can any be so simple as to conceive that the fountains should stream forth Wine, or Beer, or the woods and rivers be like Butchers-shops, or Fish-mongers stalls, where they might have things taken to their hands. If thou canst not live without such things, and hast no means to procure the one, and wilt not take pains for the other, nor hast ability to employ others for thee, rest where thou art: for as a proud heart, a dainty tooth, a beggars purse, and an idle hand, be here intolerable, so that person that hath these qualities there, is much more abominable. If therefore God hath given thee a heart to undertake such courses, upon such grounds as bear thee out in all difficulties, *viz.* his glory as a principal, and all other outward good things but as accessories, which peradventure thou shalt enjoy, and it may be not: then thou wilt with true comfort and thankfulness receive the least of his mercies; whereas on the contrary, men deprive themselves of much happiness, being senseless of greater blessings, and through prejudice smother up the love and bounty of God, whose name be ever glorified in us, and by us, now and evermore. *Amen.*

FINIS.

[59]

A Postscript.

If any man desire a more ample relation of the State of this Country, before such time as this present relation taketh place, I refer them to the two former printed books: The one published by the President and Council *for* New-England,[110] *and the other gathered by the Inhabitants of this Present Plantation at* Plimoth *in* New-England:[111] *Both which books are to be sold by* John Bellamy, *at his shop at the three golden Lions in Corne-hill near the Royal Exchange.*

A brief Relation of a credible intelligence of the present
estate of VIRGINIA.

At the earnest entreaty of some of my much respected friends, I have added to the former Discourse, a Relation of such things as were credibly reported at *Plimoth* in *New-England* in *September* last past, concerning the present estate of *Virginia*. And because men may doubt how we should have intelligence of their Affairs, being we are so far distant, I will therefore satisfy the doubtful therein. Captain *Francis West* being in *New-England* about the latter end of *May* past, sailed from thence to *Virginia*, and returned in *August:* In *September* the same Ship and Company being discharged by him at *Damarins*-Cove, came to *New-Plimoth*, where upon our earnest enquiry after the state of *Virginia* since that bloody slaughter committed by the *Indians* upon our friends and Country-men,[112] the

---

110. See *Brief Relation of the Discovery.*
111. See *Relation or Journal.*
112. Winslow refers to the 1622 attack on colonists in Virginia.

whole ships Company agreed in this; *Viz.* That upon all occasions they chased the *Indians* to and fro, insomuch, as they sued daily unto the *English* for peace, who for the present would not admit of any; That Sr *George Early*, &c. was at that present employed upon service against them; That amongst many others, *Opachancano*[113] the chief Emperour was [)(2] supposed to be slain, his son also was killed at the same time. And though by reason of these fore-named broils in the fore-part of the year, the *English* had under-gone great want of food, yet through Gods mercy there was never more shew of plenty, having as much and as good Corn on the ground as ever they had; neither was the hopes of their *Tobacco*-crop inferiour to that of their Corn: so that the Planters were never more full of encouragement, which I pray God long to continue, and so to direct both them and us, as his glory may be the principal aim and end of all our Actions, and that for his mercies sake,

AMEN.

FINIS.

---

113. Opachancano, also spelled Opechancanough, was the brother of Wahunsenacawh and succeeded his brother as leader of the Powhatans. See Allen, *Pocahontas: Medicine Woman*, 335.

Part II
RELATED TEXTS

Section 1: Captives and Emissaries

From *The Voyages of Giovanni da Verrazzano, 1524–1528*, ed. Lawrence C. Wroth (New Haven: Yale University Press, 1970), 135–36.

The Italian explorer Giovanni da Verrazzano traveled up the North American coast from the Florida peninsula to Newfoundland, probably searching for a sea passage to Asia. He wrote one of the earliest accounts of the land that would later be called New England and its peoples in his report to the French king François I, who had granted Verrazzano permission and ships to explore North America. The excerpt below details his encounter with Native Americans, probably at what is now Martha's Vineyard, Mass., or Block Island, R.I. Verrazzano took Native captives back to Europe, a practice English travelers would continue in the late sixteenth and early seventeenth centuries. In doing so, he was probably following Spanish precedent: on his first voyage, Christopher Columbus had taken numerous captives from the Caribbean.

We left this place and continued to follow the coast, which we found veered to the east. All along it we saw great fires because of the numerous inhabitants; we anchored off the shore, since there was no harbor, and because we needed water we sent the small boat ashore with xxv men. The sea along the coast was churned up by enormous waves because of the open beach, and so it was impossible to put anyone ashore without endangering the boat. We saw many people on the beach making various friendly signs, and beckoning us ashore; and there I saw a magnificent deed, as Your Majesty will hear. We sent one of our young sailors swimming ashore to take the people some trinkets, such as little bells, mirrors, and other trifles, and when he came within four fathoms of them, he

threw them the goods and tried to turn back, but he was so tossed about
by the waves that he was carried up onto the beach half dead. Seeing this,
the native people immediately ran up; they took him by the head, the legs,
and arms and carried him some distance away. Whereupon the youth,
realizing he was being carried away like this, was seized with terror, and
began to utter loud cries. They answered him in their language to show
him he should not be afraid. Then they placed him on the ground in the
sun, at the foot of a small hill, and made gestures of great admiration,
looking at the whiteness of his flesh and examining him from head to foot.
They took off his shirt and shoes and hose, leaving him naked, then made
a huge fire next to him, placing him near the heat. When the sailors in the
boat saw this, they were filled with terror, as always when something new
occurs, and thought the people wanted to roast him for food.[1] After remaining with them for a while, he regained his strength, and showed them
by signs that he wanted to return to the ship. With the greatest kindness,
they accompanied him to the sea, holding him close and embracing him;
and then to reassure him, they withdrew to a high hill and stood watch-
ing him until he was in the boat. The youth learned the following about
these people: they are dark in color like the other [tribes],[2] their skin is
very glossy, they are of medium height, their faces are more clear-cut, their
body and other limbs much more delicate and much less powerful, but
they are more quick-witted. He saw nothing else. We left this place,[3] still
following the coast which veered somewhat to the north, and after fifty

---

    1. This scene is similar to one recounted by Amerigo Vespucci of his third voyage to
the Caribbean. In Vespucci's account, the explorers sent a young "Christian" to the Natives
to reassure them of the travelers' good intentions. The Natives allegedly responded by
tearing him to pieces and eating him. See Vespucci, *Letters of Amerigo Vespucci*, 38. On
European accounts of Native Americans as cannibals, see Hulme, *Colonial Encounters*,
esp. chap. 1.
    2. This word, and the others in brackets in this selection, were added by Lawrence
C. Wroth, the twentieth-century editor of Verrazzano's account.
    3. [Verrazzano's note] *We called it 'Annunciata' from the day of arrival, and found there
an isthmus one mile wide and about two hundred miles long, in which we could see the eastern
sea from the ship, halfway between west [originally 'east'] and north. This is doubtless the one
which goes around the tip of India, China, and Cathay. We sailed along this isthmus, hoping
all the time to find some strait ['to the end of' crossed out] or real promontory where the land
might end to the north, and we could reach those blessed shores of Cathay. This isthmus was
named by the discoverer 'Varazanio,' just as all the land we found was called 'Francesca' after
our Francis.*

leagues we reached another land which seemed much more beautiful and full of great forests. We anchored there, and with xx men we penetrated about two leagues inland, to find that the people had fled in terror into the forests. Searching everywhere, we met with a very old woman and a young girl of xviii to xx years, who had hidden in the grass in fear. The old woman had two little girls whom she carried on her shoulders, and clinging to her neck a boy—they were all about eight years old. The young woman also had three children, but all girls. When we met them, they began to shout. The old woman made signs to us that the men had fled to the woods. We gave her some of our food to eat, which she accepted with great pleasure; the young woman refused everything and threw it angrily to the ground. We took the boy from the old woman to carry back to France, and we wanted to take the young woman, who was very beautiful and tall, but it was impossible to take her to the sea because of the loud cries she uttered. And as we were a long way from the ship and had to pass through several woods, we decided to leave her behind, and took only the boy. We found these people whiter than the previous ones; they were dressed in certain grasses that hang from the branches of the trees and which they weave with different threads of wild hemp. Their heads are bare and of the same shape as the others. On the whole they live on pulses,[4] which are abundant and different from ours in color and size, but are excellent and have a delicious taste; otherwise they live by hunting fish and birds, which they catch with bows and snares. They make [the bows] of hard wood, the arrows of reeds, and at the point they put the bones of fish and other animals. The wild animals here are much more ferocious than in Europe because they are continually being molested by hunters. We saw many of their little boats made out of a single tree, twenty feet long and four feet wide, which are put together without stone, iron, or any other kind of metal. For in the whole country, in the area of two hundred leagues that we covered, we did not see a single stone of any kind. They use the fourth element [fire] and burn the wood as much as necessary to hollow out the boat: they do the same for the stern and the prow so that when it sails it can plow through the waves of the sea. The land is like the previous one in situation, fertility, and beauty; the woods

---

4. Edible seeds (such as peas or beans).

are sparse; the land is covered with different types of trees, but they are not so fragrant, since there it is more northern and cold. We saw there many vines growing wild, which climb up around the trees as they do in Cisalpine Gaul:[5] they would doubtless produce excellent wines if they were properly cultivated, for several times we found the dry fruit sweet and pleasant, not unlike our own. The people must value them, because wherever they grow, the bushes around them are removed so that the fruit can ripen better.

From James Rosier, *A True Relation of the most prosperous voyage made this present year 1605, by Captain George Waymouth, in the discovery of the land of Virginia* (London, 1605), C4r–C4v, E2v–E3r.

James Rosier and George Waymouth traveled to what is now Maine to scout locations for a colony for Catholic settlers, but found, upon their return to England, that their supporters had lost interest in the project. A Cambridge graduate, Rosier went on the voyage as a merchant and observer for his patron, the Catholic gentleman Thomas Arundell. He recorded his impressions in his *True Relation*, which was published upon his return in 1605 and then excerpted in 1624 in Samuel Purchas's *Purchas his Pilgrims*.

The English travelers kidnapped and returned to London with five Abenaki men, whom they delivered to the colonial investor and promoter Ferdinando Gorges. Along with John Smith, Gorges was one of the earliest promoters of colonization in New England. He took the Abenaki captives into his household and attempted to use their knowledge of New England to develop plans for colonization.

About eight a clock this day we went on shore with our boats, to fetch aboard water and wood, our Captain leaving word with the Gunner in the Ship, by discharging a musket, to give notice if they espied any Canoe coming: which they did about ten a clock. He therefore being careful they

---

5. A Roman province until 41 BC, eventually merged into Roman Italy.

should be kindly entreated, requested me to go aboard, intending with dispatch to make what haste after he possibly could. When I came to the ship, there were two Canoes, and in either of them three Savages; of whom two were below at the fire, the other stayed in their Canoes about the ship; and because we could not entice them aboard, we gave them a Can of peas and bread, which they carried to the shore to eat. But one of them brought back our Can presently and stayed aboard with the other two; for he being young, of a ready capacity, and one we most desired to bring with us into England, had received exceeding kind usage at our hands, and was therefore much delighted in our company. When our Captain was come, we consulted how to catch the other three at shore, which we performed thus.

[6]We manned the light horseman[7] with 7 or 8 men, one standing before carried our box of Merchandise, as we were wont when I went to traffic with them, and a platter of peas, which meat they loved: but before we were landed, one of them (being too suspiciously fearful of his own good) withdrew himself into the wood. The other two met us on the shore side, to receive the peas, with whom we went up the Cliff to their fire and sat down with them, and whiles we were discussing how to catch the third man who was gone, I opened the box, and showed them trifles to exchange, thinking thereby to have banished fear from the other, and drawn him to return: but when we could not, we used little delay, but suddenly laid hands upon them. And it was as much as five or six of us could do to get them into the light horseman. For they were strong and so naked as our best hold was by their long hair on their heads: and we would have been very loath to have done them any hurt, which of necessity we had been constrained to have done if we had attempted them in a multitude, which we must and would, rather than have wanted them, being a matter of great importance for the full accomplement of our voyage.[8]

Thus we shipped five Savages, two Canoes, with all their bows and arrows.

[...]

---

6. Rosier's margin note: Our manner of taking the Savages.
7. A now obsolete term for a light boat. See *Oxford English Dictionary*, 2nd ed., s.v., "light horseman," n. 3.
8. Rosier's margin note: We caught five Savages, two Canoes, and their bows and arrows.

Further, I have thought fit here to add some things worthy to be regarded, which we have observed from the Savages since we took them.

First, although at the time when we surprised them, they made their
best resistance, not knowing our purpose, nor what we were, nor how we
meant to use them; yet after perceiving by their kind usage we intended
them no harm, they have never since seemed discontented with us, but
very tractable, loving, & willing by their best means to satisfy us in anything we demand of them, by words or signs for their understanding:
neither have they at any time been at the least discord among themselves;
insomuch as we have not seen them angry, but merry; and so kind, as if
you give any thing to one of them, he will distribute part to every one of
the rest.

We have brought them to understand some English, and we understand much of their language; so as we are able to ask them many things.
And this we have observed, that if we show them any thing, and ask them
if they have it in their country, they will tell you if they have it, and the use
of it, the difference from ours in bigness, color, or form: but if they have
it not, be it a thing never so precious, they will deny the knowledge of it.

From Ferdinando Gorges, "A Description of New England,"
in *America Painted to the Life. The True History Of The Spaniards
Proceedings in the Conquests of the Indians . . . More especially,
an absolute Narrative of the North parts of America, and of the Discoveries
and Plantations of our English in Virginia, New-England, and Barbados*
(London, 1659), 19–20.

A soldier who fought in England's sixteenth-century wars against
Spain, Gorges later became captain and commander of Plymouth
Harbour, England. He funded several failed attempts to settle the
coast of New England before receiving a royal patent in 1620 for
territory between what is now Philadelphia and Newfoundland. He
developed this area primarily by granting sections of land to some
settlers and by financing fishing stations. Gorges never traveled
to America himself, although he worked extensively with several

Native captives, including Tisquantum, in hopes of learning about and profiting from the New World's resources.[9] In this selection, Gorges described the return of Epenow, the Martha's Vineyard sachem, to New England, referenced Thomas Hunt's kidnapping of Tisquantum, and indicated his ongoing plans for colonization in New England. Gorges's description of New England was published in a collection of his writings about the New World, compiled by his grandson, Ferdinando Gorges Jr.

[N]ot long after Captain *Hobson*[10] and others were set out with very great preparations, and with them two *Savages*[11] which had been detained for some time in *England*, whom they thought to make use of, the better to draw the rest of the Natives to their commerce, but in regard that a little before their arrival, a certain *English-man* named *Hunt*, had brought away from that place 24 of the *Savages* whom he had by treachery, and under pretence of friendship enticed into his Ship, and as it came afterwards to be known, had sold them to the *Spaniards* in the straits of *Gibraltar*, the *Savages* from thence contracted so great an animosity toward the *English*, that Captain *Hobson* was constrained to return without doing any thing. In the year 1614 Captain *John Smith* was sent (to fish for Whales, and to seek for Mines of gold and silver) who landed upon the Island of *Monahiggan*,[12] he found some store of Whales, but not those kind of Whales which afford so much profit by reason of their Oil; the next year being sent again, he fell into the hands of *French Pirates*, who detain'd him Prisoner for a certain time, nevertheless one of the *Savages* which *Hunt* had sold to the *Spaniards*, happening to fall into the hands of the *English*, they again conceived new hopes, and having with much difficulty obtain'd a new Patent from the King, they a little after brought a new Colony into those parts.[13]

---

9. See Clark, "Gorges, Sir Ferdinando (1568–1647)."
10. Thomas Hobson was a captain on several voyages funded by Gorges.
11. One of these "savages" is probably Epenow, the Martha's Vineyard sachem.
12. The island Monhegan, near what is now Maine.
13. Gorges may be referring to his own royal patent of 1620.

From Phenehas Pratt, *A Declaration Of The Affairs Of The English People That First Inhabited New England* (1662).

Phenehas (or Phineas) Pratt, the Wessagusset colonist who traveled to Plimoth with news of the Massachusetts' plan to attack the colonies, did not publish his account; instead, he presented it in manuscript form to the Massachusetts General Court in 1662, as part of a petition for land and financial assistance. Pratt argued that his sufferings in the early 1620s and the fact that he was among the first colonists to settle in New England qualified him for aid. As a result, he received three hundred acres; he again requested but was denied assistance from the court in 1668.

The "Declaration" offers Pratt's short history of Wessagusset colony, including interactions between the Wessagusset men and the Massachusetts, who lived nearby. This section includes Pratt's report of Massachusett accounts of French colonists, whom they took as captives.

Then we [the colonists who settled at Wessagusset] perceived that on the south part of the Bay were fewest of the natives of the Country Dwelling there. We thought best to begin our plantation, but fearing A great Company of Savages we being but 10 men thought it best to see if our friends were Living at Plimoth. Then sailing Along the Coast not knowing the harbor, they shot off a piece of Ordnance & at our coming Ashore, they entertained us with 3 volley of shots. Their second ship was Returned for England before we Came to them. We asked them where the Rest of our friends were that came in the first ship. They said that God had taken them Away by death & that before their second ship came they were so distressed with sickness that they, fearing the savages should know it, had set up their sick men with their muskets upon their Rests & their backs Leaning Against trees. At this Time one or two of them went with us in our vessel to the place of fishing to buy victuals. 8 or 9 weeks after this two of our ships Arrived at Plimoth, the lesser of our 3 ships continued in the Country with us. Then we made haste to settle our plantation in the

Massachusetts bay, our Number being near sixty men. At the same time there was a great plague Among the savages & as them selves told us half their people died thereof. The Natives called the place of our plantation Wessagusscus—Near unto it is a town of Later Time Called Weymouth. The Savages seemed to be good friends with us while they feared us, but when they saw famine prevail they began to insult as appeareth by the sequel. For one of their Pnieses or Chief men, Called Pexworth,[14] employed himself to Learn to speak English, observing all things for his bloody ends. He told me he Loved English men very well, but he Loved me best of all. Then he said, you say French men do not love you but I will tell you what we have done to them. There was a ship broken by a storm. They saved most of their goods & hid it in the Ground. We made them tell us where it was. Then we made them our servants. They wept much. When we parted [with] them we gave them such meat as our dogs ate. One of them had a Book he would often Read in. We Asked him what his Book said. He answered, It saith there will a people, like French men, Come into this Country and drive you all a way, & now we think you are they. We took Away their Clothes. They lived but a little while. One of them Lived Longer than the Rest for he had a good master & gave him a wife. He is now dead, but hath a son Alive, An other Ship Come into the bay with much goods to Truck, then I said to the Sachem I will tell you how you shall have all for nothing. Bring all our Canoes & all our Beaver & a great many men, but no bow nor Arrow Clubs, nor Hatchets, but knives under the skins that About our Lines.[15] Throw up much Beaver upon their Deck sell it very Cheap & when I give the word, thrust your knives in the French mens Bellies. Thus we killed them all. But Monsieur Finch Master of their ship—being wounded, Leaped into the hold. We bid him come up but he would not. Then we cut their Cable & the ship went Ashore & lay upon her side & slept there. Finch Came up & we killed him. Then our Sachem divided their goods & fired their Ship & it made a very great fire. Some of our Company Asked them how long it was Ago since they first see ships, they said they could not tell but they had

---

14. Winslow spelled this name "Pecksuot."
15. Probably trap lines.

heard men say the first ship that they see, seemed to be a floating Island as they supposed broken off from the main Land wrapped together with the Roots of Trees with some trees upon it. They went to it with their Canoes, but seeing men & hearing guns, they made haste to be gone.

Section 2: Disease and Disorder

From John Smith, *A Description of New England: Or The Observations, And discoveries, of Captain John Smith (Admiral of that Country) in the North of America . . . With the proof of the present benefit this Country affords; whither this present year, 1616, eight voluntary Ships are gone to make further trial* (London, 1616), 26–27.

By March 1614, when he first traveled to New England, John Smith had already helped to establish a colony at Jamestown, in Virginia, and had also served as its governor for about two years. While he is probably best known today for his brief description of the Powhatan woman Pocahontas, in the seventeenth century Smith gave New England its present name and was the most vocal promoter of colonization in that region, even though he never established a colony there. This selection provides one of the first English descriptions of the areas that are now known as Massachusetts Bay and Plymouth. Smith's account of thousands of inhabitants contrasts with later accounts (excerpted in section 3), which describe populations reduced by the 1616–1619 epidemics.

The Isles of *Mattahunts*[16] are on the West side of this Bay, where are many Isles, and questionless good harbors: and then the Country of the *Massachusetts*, which is the Paradise of all those parts: for, here are many Isles all planted with corn; groves, mulberries, savage gardens, and good harbors: the Coast is for the most part, high clayie sandy cliffs. The Sea Coast as you pass, shows you all along large corn fields, and great troupes of well proportioned people: but the *French* having remained here near six weeks,

---

16. Smith may have been referring to Nahant, Mass. See Lewis, *History of Lynn*, 43.

left nothing, for us to take occasion to examine the inhabitants relations, *viz.* if there be near three thousand people upon these Isles; and that the River doth pierce many days journeys the entrails of that Country. We found the people in those parts very kind; but in their fury no less valiant. For, upon a quarrel we had with one of them, he only with three others, crossed the harbor of *Quonahassit*[17] to certain rocks whereby we must pass; and there let fly their arrows for our shot, till we were out of danger.

Then come you to *Accomack*[18] an excellent good harbor, good land; and no want of any thing, but industrious people. After much kindness, upon a small occasion, we fought also with forty or fifty of those: though some were hurt, and some slain; yet within an hour after, they became friends.[19]

From Ferdinando Gorges, "A Description of New England," in *America Painted to the Life* (London, 1659), 26–28.

This selection includes travelers' accounts of Native responses to the 1616–1619 epidemics. It is likely that Ferdinando Gorges Jr. copied these reports from Edward Johnson's *History of New-England* (also known as *Wonder-Working Providence*), since the description of the comet and the devastation caused by the diseases follows (and at times replicates) Johnson's text. *History of New-England* was published in London in 1653 (printed with a date of 1654) and, after selling poorly, was rebound and sold with Gorges's writings.

[T]he *Indians* about that time beheld to their great amazement that blazing Comet (so much noted in *Europe*)[20] which appear'd after Sun-setting

---

17. *Quonahassit* refers to what is now Norfolk County, Mass.; Smith's reference to the harbor may refer to Massachusetts Bay. Smith seems to have traveled south from Nahant toward Cape Cod. *Quonahassit* is a Natick word for a "long rock place" or a "fishing promontory." See Huden, *Indian Place Names*, 210.

18. Plimoth. See Smith, *General History* (1632), 205.

19. Smith reported several violent confrontations with Natives in New England; according to him, the encounters eventually ended in peace. See Salisbury, *Manitou and Providence*, 99–100.

20. Europeans reported seeing a comet in 1618. See Bainbridge, *Astronomical Description* and *Controversy on the Comets of 1618*.

in their Horizon South-west for the space of 30 sleeps, (for so they reckon their days) after which uncouth sight, they expected some strange things to follow, the whole Nation of the *Massachusetts* having been a little before that affrighted with the arrival of a ship of ours in their bay, wondering exceedingly what strange creature it should be, when they beheld a great thing moving toward them upon the Water, especially when having let fly their arrows at it out of their Cannons, thinking to have killed it, the Master caused a piece of Ordnance to be fired, whereby the poor *Indians* struck with a Panic fear hasted to the shore, but when our men appeared and produced their copper Kettles, they were by degrees invited to trade with us for Beaver skins; the Summer after the blazing star (which moved from the East to West) even a little before the *English* removed from *Holland* to *Plimoth* in *New-England*, there befell a very great mortality among the *Indians*, the greatest that had ever happened in the memory of man, or been taken notice of by tradition, laying desolate the East, and by the Northern parts the County of *Pockanckie*,[21] *Agissawamg*,[22] the *Abarginny*[23] men consisting of *Wippanaps*, *Tarantines*[24] and *The Sagamore-ships*, or petty Kingdoms of the *Massachusetts* the *Niantics*, *Narragansetts*, & *Pecods*,[25] their Powwows or Doctors were amazed to see their Wigwams or streets lie full of dead bodies, and neither *Squantam* their good, nor *Abbamoch* their bad God could help them, which very much facilitated the landing of the *English* not long after in *Plimoth* Plantation, who coming but with a handful of men found little or no resistance, being only sent to keep possession for the brethren who arrived Eight days after, when the Natives appearing with their bows, and arrows let fly their long shafts among them; but one Captain *Miles Standish* with his fowling piece shot the stoutest *Sachem*, among the *Indians* upon the right arm as he was reaching an arrow from his quiver, whereupon they

---

21. Probably Pokanoket, where Massasoit's people lived.

22. Perhaps Agawam, now Hampden County, Mass., or Plymouth County, Mass. Agawam is a Nipmuck word for "low land," or a "place to unload canoes." See Huden, *Indian Place Names*, 19.

23. Several early colonists employed the term "Aberginian" (perhaps a translation of Abenaki) to refer to Natives north of Massachusetts Bay. The "Wippanaps" were included in this group. See Hodge, *Handbook of American Indians*, 1.

24. The Tarrantines, now known as the Mi'kmaq.

25. Probably the Pequots.

all fled away with great speed through the woods and thickets,[26] the same year the Merchant Adventurers in *England* sent forth store of Servants to provide against the wants of that desert place, amongst whom came over a mixed multitude, who settled themselves in the bosom of Cape *Anne*, now called *Gloucester*, and with them came over Mr. *John Indicate*[27] as Governor in that place, they immediately began to build a town which is now called *Salem*.

From Ferdinando Gorges, *A Brief Narration Or The Original Undertakings Of The Advancement Of Plantations Into the Parts of America. Especially, Showing the beginning, progress and continuance of that of New-England. Written by the right Worshipful, Sir Ferdinando Gorges, Knight and Governour of the Fort and Island of Plymouth in Devonshire* (London, 1658), 12.

This selection includes one of the only printed eyewitness accounts of the epidemics. Gorges received the account from one of his men, Richard Vines. The *Brief Narration* was bound with *America, Painted to the Life* in 1659.

[T]hough as yet I was forced to hire Men to stay there the Winter Quarter at extreme rates, and not without danger, for that the War had consumed the Bashaba,[28] and the most of the great Sagamores,[29] with such Men of Action as followed them, and those that remained were sore

---

26. Gorges may be referring to an exchange in the winter of 1620–21 between the Plimoth colonists and some Algonquians, in which the colonists first believed the Natives' voices to be those of wolves. *A Relation or Journal* states that Standish shot at a man believed to be the Natives'"Captain" (probably a pniese), but the man withstood three shots from one of the colonists' guns, and then, seeing that one of the colonists had a clean shot at him, ran away before the colonist could fire. See *Relation or Journal*, 18–19.
27. John Endecott. See Bremer,"Endecott, John (d. 1665)."
28. A Penobscot Abenaki sachem (whose name is also spelled "Bashabes"), who traded with French explorer Samuel de Champlain. His men traded with and were captured by George Waymouth and James Rosier. See the selection from Rosier in section 1.
29. Another word for sachem.

afflicted with the Plague,[30] for that the Country was in a manner left void
of Inhabitants; Notwithstanding, *Vines*[31] and the rest with him that lay
in the Cabins with those People that died some more, some less, mightily,
(blessed be *GOD* for it) not one of them ever felt their heads to ache while
they stayed there; and this course I held some years together, but nothing to my private profit, for what I got one way I spent another, so that I
began to grow weary of that business as not for my turn till better times.

From Thomas Dermer, "To his Worshipful Friend M. Samuel Purchas,
Preacher of the Word, at the Church a Little within *Ludgate, London,*"
in *Purchas His Pilgrims, in Five Books . . . The Fourth Part,*
ed. Samuel Purchas (London, 1625), 1778–79.

Thomas Dermer traveled several times to New England, with John
Smith in 1614 and later in the employment of Ferdinando Gorges.
Along with Richard Vines, Dermer provided a report of the epidemics of 1616–1619, a description that was printed by colonial promoter and clergyman Samuel Purchas.

SIR,

*It was the nineteenth of May, before I was fitted for my discovery, when
from* Monahiggan[32] *I set sail in an open Pinnace of five ton, for the Island I
told you of. I passed alongst the Coast where I found some ancient Plantations,
not long since populous now utterly void; in other places a remnant remains,
but not free of sickness. Their disease the Plague, for we might perceive the
sores of some that had escaped, who described the spots of such as usually die.*

---

30. Like Gorges's men, Morton and Dermer also described the Natives' disease as
"the plague" (see selections below). However, it is unlikely that the illness was the bubonic plague, as that disease probably could not have survived the journey across the
Atlantic. Scholars remain uncertain regarding the identity of the disease. See note 79 in
the introduction.

31. Richard Vines, one of the men Gorges employed to explore New England. He
settled in New England, near the Saco River, in 1630; he worked as agent and deputy
governor for Gorges in Maine. In 1646, Vines relocated to Barbados, where he had a
profitable tobacco and cotton plantation. See Gragg, "Vines, Richard (1597/8–1651)."

32. Monhegan, Me.

*When I arrived at my Savages[33] native Country (finding all dead) I trav-
eled alongst a days journey Westward, to a place called* Nummastaquyt,[34]
*where finding Inhabitants, I dispatched a Messenger a days journey further
West, to* Poconaokit *which bordereth on the Sea; whence came to see me two
Kings,[35] attended with a guard of fifty armed men, who being well satisfied
with that my Savage and I discoursed unto them (being desirous of novelty)
gave me content in whatsoever I demanded, where I found that former relations were true. Here I redeemed a* Frenchman, *and afterwards another at*
Massachusett, *who three years since escaped shipwreck at the North-east of*
Cape Cod. *I must (amongst many things worthy observation) for want of
leisure, therefore hence I pass (not mentioning any place where we touched in
the way) to the Island, which we discovered the twelfth of June. Here we had
good quarter with the Savages, who likewise confirmed former reports. [. . .]
Being thus overcharged with weather, I stood alongst the coast to seek harbors,
to attend a favorable gale to recover the strait, but being a harborless Coast for
ought we could then perceive, we found no succor till we arrived betwixt Cape*
Charles *and the Main on the* East *side [of] the Bay* Chestapeak,[36] *where in
a wild Road we anchored; and the next day (the eight of September) crossed
the Bay to* Kecoughtan,[37] *where the first news struck cold to our hearts, the
general sickness over the Land. Here I resolved with all possible speed to return
in pursuit of this business; so that after a little refreshing, we recovered up the
River to* James City, *and from thence to* Cape Warde *his Plantation, where
immediately we fell to hewing of Boards for a close Deck, having found it a
most desired course to attempt as before. As we were thus laboring to effect
our purposes, it pleased almighty God (who only disposeth of the times and
seasons, wherein all works shall be accomplished) to visit us with his heavy
hand, so that at one time there were but two of us able to help the rest, my
self so sore shaken with a burning fever, that I was brought even unto deaths
door, but at length by Gods assistance escaped, and have now with the rest
almost recovered my former strength. The Winter having overtaken us (a
time on these Coasts especially) subject to gusts and fearful storms, I have now*

---

33. Tisquantum.
34. Nemasket, now in the area that is Plymouth County, Mass.
35. Massasoit and Conbatant were the sachems at Pokanoket and Nemasket, respectively; they may have been the "kings" who came to meet Dermer.
36. Chesapeake.
37. In Virginia, near what are now Hampton, Va., and the Hampton River.

resolved to choose a more temperate season, both for the general good and our own safeties. And thus I have sent you a broken discourse, though indeed very unwilling to have given any notice at all, till it had pleased God to have blessed me with a thorough search, that our eyes might have witnessed the truth. I have drawn a Plot of the Coast, which I dare not yet part with for fear of danger, let this therefore serve for confirmation of your hopes, till I can better perform my promise and your desire, for what I have spoken I can produce at least mille testes;[38] far separate, of the Sea behind them, and of Ships, which come many days journey from the West, and of the great extent of this Sea to the North and South, not knowing any bounds thereof Westward. I cease to trouble you till a better opportunity offer it self, remembering my best love, &c. I rest

From Captain MARTYN his Plantation.
   27. Decemb. 1619.   Yours to command,
                                                      THO. DERMER

From Thomas Morton, *New English Canaan or New Canaan.
Containing an Abstract of New England, Composed in three Books . . .
written by Thomas Morton* (Amsterdam, 1637), 22–24.

Thomas Morton was a gentleman and lawyer who traveled to New England in 1625 and settled at Passonagessit (now Quincy, Mass.). When the colony's leader, Captain Wollaston, left with some of the colonists for Virginia, Morton took over the plantation, renamed it Ma-re Mount, and raised a maypole in a celebration to which he invited nearby Natives (probably the Massachusetts, but possibly other tribes as well). Morton traded so successfully with New England Natives that the Plimoth colonists requested him to discontinue his transactions, complaining that he provided the Natives with guns and worrying privately that his profitable trade would hurt their own stake in trading networks. When Morton refused, Myles Standish traveled to Ma-re Mount to force him to stop trading; the Plimoth colonists banished Morton to an island,

---

38. A "thousand tests."

during which time Native people provided him with food. Plimoth insisted that he return to England, but he subsequently traveled back to New England several times. *New English Canaan* recounts Morton's conflict with the Plimoth colonists with witty accounts of their religious practices and of his encounters with New England Algonquians. In this excerpt, Morton described the evidence he observed of the 1616–1619 epidemics. He also gave another account of the Frenchmen taken captive by the Massachusetts (also described by Pratt; see section 1).

Of a great mortality that happened amongst the Natives of New England near about the time, that the English came there to plant.

It fortuned some few years, before the English came to inhabit at new Plimoth in New England; that upon some distaste given in the Massachusetts bay, by Frenchmen, then trading there with the Natives for beaver, they set upon the men, at such advantage, that they killed many of them burned their ship then riding at Anchor by an Island there, now called Peddocks Island[39] in memory of Leonard Peddock that landed there (where many wild Anckies[40] haunted that time which he thought had been tame,) distributing them unto 5. Sachems which were Lords of the several territories adjoining, they did keep them so long as they lived, only to sport themselves at them, and made these five Frenchmen[41] fetch them wood and water, which is the general work that they require of a servant, one of these five men out living the rest had learned so much of their language, as to rebuke them for their bloody deed, saying that God would be angry with them for it; and that he would in his displeasure destroy them; but the Savages (it seems boasting of their strength,) replied and said, that they were so many, that God could not kill them.

---

39. In Massachusetts Bay.
40. Possibly "Auckies," a version of "Auk." See the unnumbered footnote in Thomas Morton, "Manners and Customs of the Indians," *Old South Leaflets*, no. 87 (Boston: 1899), 14.
41. Morton's margin note: *Five Frenchmen kept by the Savages.*

But[42] contrary wise in short time after, the hand of God fell heavily upon them, with such a mortal stroke, that they died on heaps, as they lay in their houses and the living; that were able to shift for themselves would run away, & let them die, and let their Carcasses lie above the ground without burial. For in a place where many inhabited, there hath been but one left alive, to tell what became of the rest, the living being (as it seems) not able to bury the dead, they were left for Crows, Kites,[43] and vermin to prey upon.[44] And the bones and skulls upon the several places of their habitations, made such a spectacle after my coming into those parts, that as I travailed in that Forest, near the Massachusetts, it seemed to me a new found Golgotha.

But otherwise it is the custom of those Indian people, to bury their dead ceremoniously, and carefully, and then to abandon that place, because they have no desire the place should put them in mind of mortality: and this mortality was not ended, when the Brownists[45] of new Plimoth were settled at Patuxet in New England, and by all likelihood the sickness that these Indians died of, was the Plague, as by conference with them since my arrival, and habitation in those parts, I have learned. And by this means there is as yet but a small number of Savages in New England to that, which hath been in former time, and the place is made so much the more fit,[46] for the English Nation to inhabit in, and erect in it Temples to the glory of God.

From Robert Cushman, *A Sermon Preached at Plimoth in New England . . . Written in the year 1621* (London, 1622), 10–12.

Robert Cushman was one of the Plimoth colonists' elders, or spiritual leaders; he had been part of the Separatist church at Leiden

---

42. Morton's margin note: *The Plague fell on the Indians.*
43. A bird of prey.
44. Morton's margin note: *The living not able to bury the dead.*
45. "Brownist" was an early term for the Separatists. It referred to Robert Brown, who criticized the Church of England and its bishops' authority and who was imprisoned and persecuted for his dissenting views.
46. Morton's margin note: 2. *Sam.* 24.

since 1609. Cushman also served for a time as the colonists' agent, or representative, to investors in England. He traveled to New England in November 1621, bringing thirty-five additional colonists on the *Fortune*. He probably returned to England with the letters and reports that comprised the *Relation or Journal of the Beginning and Proceedings of the English Plantation Settled at Plimoth in New England;* in addition, he published a sermon he had delivered at Plimoth.[47] These documents comprised some of the first publications about the colony. In the selection from the sermon below, Cushman discussed concerns regarding the effects of the New World and its hardships on colonists. He compared the sin of selfishness or "self-love" to a disease that only a divine physician could heal; in this way, he warned the colonists not to imitate the ungodly behavior of the Jamestown settlers, some of whom reportedly hoarded food for themselves or went so far as to resort to cannibalism when food supplies were depleted.

A Sermon Preached at *Plimoth*, in *New-England*.

If God see[48] this disease of self-love so dangerous in us, then it standeth us all in hand to suspect our selves, and so to seek out the root of this disease, that it may be cured. If a learned Physician,[49] shall see by our countenance and eye, that we have some dangerous disease growing on us, our hearts will smite us, and we will bethink our selves, where the most grief lieth, and how it should come, whether with cold, heat, surfeit, overflowing of blood, or through grief, melancholy, or any such way, and every man will bestir himself to get rid of it, and will prevent all ways that feed the disease, and cherish all courses that would destroy it.

Now, how much more ought we to bestir ourselves, for this matter of self-love, since God himself hath cast all our waters,[50] and felt all our

---

47. See Bradford, *Of Plymouth Plantation*, 38, n. 3.
48. Cushman's margin note: *Ver 2.*
49. Cushman's margin note: *Simile.*
50. The process, usually undertaken by physicians, of inspecting or analyzing the patient's urine, or "water," to diagnose disease.

pulses, and pronounced us all dangerously sick of this disease? believe it, God cannot lie, nor be deceived; He that made the heart, doth not he know it? Let every mans heart smite him, and let him fall to examination of himself, and see first, whether he love not riches and worldly wealth too much, whether his heart be not too jocund at the coming of it in, and too heavy at the going of it out, for if you find it so, there is great danger; if thou canst not buy as if thou[51] possessed not, and use this world as thou used it not, thou art sick and had need to look to it. So, if thou lovest[52] thine ease and pleasure, see whether thou canst be content to receive[53] at Gods hands evil as well as good; whether thou have learned as well to abound as to want, as well to endure hard labor, as to live at ease; and art as willing to go to the house of mourning as to the house of mirth;[54] for, else, out of doubt, thou lovest thy carnal pleasure and ease too much. [...]

It is reported,[55] that there are many men gone to that other Plantation in *Virginia*, which, whilst they lived in England, seemed very religious, zealous, and conscionable; and have now lost even the sap of grace, and edge to all goodness; and are become mere worldlings: This testimony I believe to be partly true, and amongst many causes of it, this self-love is not the least; It is indeed a matter of some commendations for a man to remove himself out of a thronged place into a wide wilderness; to take in hand so long and dangerous a journey, to be an instrument to carry the Gospel and humanity among the brutish heathen; but there may be many goodly shows and glosses and yet a pad in the straw,[56] men may make a great appearance of respect unto God, and yet but dissemble with him, having their own lusts carrying them: and, out of doubt, men that have taken in hand hither to come, out of discontentment, in regard of their estates in England; and aiming at great matters here, affecting it to be Gentlemen, landed men, or hoping for office, place, dignity, or fleshly liberty; let the show be what it will, the substance is nought, and that bird of self-love which was hatched at home, if it be not looked to, will eat

51. Cushman's margin note: 1 *Cor.* 7.30.31.
52. Cushman's margin note: *Job* 2.10.
53. Cushman's margin note: *Phil.* 2.10.
54. Cushman's margin note: *Eccle* 7.6.
55. Cushman's margin note: *A Fair Warning.*
56. Cushman's margin note: *Psal.* 78.5.7.

out the life of all grace and goodness: and though men have escaped the danger of the sea, and that cruel mortality, which swept away so many of our loving friends and brethren; yet except they purge out this self-love, a worse mischief is prepared for them: And who knoweth whether God in mercy have delivered those just men which here departed,[57] from the evils to come; and from unreasonable men, in whom there neither was, nor is, any comfort but grief, sorrow, affliction, and misery, till they cast out this spawn of self-love.

---

57. Cushman's margin note: *Isa.* 57.1.

Section 3: Compromise and Conflict

From William Bradford and Edward Winslow, *A Relation Or Journal of the beginning and proceedings of the English Plantation settled at Plimoth in New England, by certain English adventurers both Merchants and others* (London, 1622), 35–38.

This selection details the meeting that the Pokanoket Wampanoags initiated with the Plimoth colonists, in the spring after their arrival at Patuxet. In addition, the selection describes the agreement the Pokanoket Wampanoag and the colonists made, also in spring 1621.

Thursday the 22. of *March,* was a very fair warm day. About noon we met again about our public business, but we had scarce been an hour together, but *Samoset*[58] came again, and *Squanto,*[59] the only native of *Patuxet,* where we now inhabit, who was one of the twenty Captives that by *Hunt* were carried away, and had been in *England* & dwelt in *Cornehill* with master *John Slanie* a Merchant,[60] and could speak a little English, with three others, and they brought with them some few skins to truck and some red Herrings newly taken and dried, but not salted, and signified unto us, that their great Sagamore *Masasoyt* was hard by, with *Quadequina* his brother, and all their men. They could not well express in English what they would, but after an hour the King came to the top of an hill over against us, and had in his train sixty men, that we could well behold them, and they us: we were not willing to send our governor to

---

58. An Abenaki man who had traded with the English in what is now Maine.

59. Squanto was also known as Tisquantum.

60. John Slanie, or Slany, as his name is sometimes spelled, was treasurer of the Newfoundland Company. Cornehill (or Cornhill) was the location of important guilds and shops (including one of the shops that sold *Good News*) as well as the houses of wealthy merchants. See Bailyn, *New England Merchants,* 36–37.

them, and they unwilling to come to us, so *Squanto* went again unto him, who brought word that we should send one to parley with him, which we did, which was *Edward Winslow*, to know his mind, and to signify the mind and will of our governor, which was to have trading and peace with him. We sent to the King a pair of Knives, and a Copper Chain, with a Jewel at it. To *Quadequina* we sent likewise a Knife and a Jewel to hang in his ear, and withal a Pot of strong water, a good quantity of Biscuit, and some butter, which were all willingly accepted: our Messenger made a speech unto him, that King JAMES saluted him with words of love and Peace, and did accept of him as his Friend and Ally, and that our Governor desired to see him and to truck with him, and to confirm a Peace with him, as his next neighbor: he liked well of the speech and heard it attentively, though the Interpreters did not well express it; after he had eaten and drunk himself, and given the rest to his company, he looked upon our messengers sword and armor which he had on, with intimation of his desire to buy it, but on the other side, our messenger showed his unwillingness to part with it: In the end he left him in the custody of *Quadequina* his brother, and came over the brook; and some twenty men following him, leaving all their Bows and Arrows behind them. We kept six or seven as hostages for our messenger; Captain *Standish* and master *Williamson*[61] met the King at the brook, with half a dozen Musketeers, they saluted him and he them, so one going over, the one on the one side, and the other on the other, conducted him to a house then in building, where we placed a green Rug, and three or four Cushions, then instantly came our Governor[62] with Drum and Trumpet after him, and some few Musketeers. After salutations, our Governor kissing his hand, the King kissed him, and so they sat down. The Governor called for some strong water, and drunk to him, and he drunk a great draught that made him sweat all the while after, he called for a little fresh meat, which the King did eat willingly, and did give his followers. Then they treated of Peace, which was;

    1. That neither he nor any of his should injure or do hurt to any of our people.[63]

---

61. Possibly Thomas Williams or a misprint for Isaac Allerton. See Young, *Chronicles of the Pilgrim Fathers*, 192, n.1.
62. John Carver.
63. Margin note: The agreements of peace between us and Massasoyt.

2. And if any of his did hurt to any of ours, he should send the offender, that we might punish him.

3. That if any of our Tools were taken away when our people were at work, he should cause them to be restored, and if ours did any harm to any of his, we would do the like to them.

4. If any did unjustly war against him, we would aid him; If any did war against us, he should aid us.

5. He should send to his neighbor Confederates, to certify them of this, that they might not wrong us, but might be likewise comprised in the conditions of Peace.

6. That when their men came to us, they should leave their Bows and Arrows behind them, as we should do our Pieces[64] when we came to them.

Lastly, that doing thus, King JAMES would esteem of him as his friend and Ally: all which the King seemed to like well, and it was applauded of his followers, all the while he sat by the Governor he trembled for fear: In his person he is a very lusty[65] man, in his best years, an able body, grave of countenance, and spare of speech: In his Attire little or nothing differing from the rest of his followers, only in a great Chain of white bone Beads about his neck,[66] and at it behind his neck, hangs a little bag of Tobacco, which he drank and gave us to drink; his face was painted with a sad red like murry,[67] and oiled both head and face, that he looked greasily: All his followers likewise, were in their faces, in part or in whole painted, some black, some red, some yellow, and some white, some with crosses, and other Antick works, some had skins on them, and some naked, all strong, tall, all men in appearance: so after all was done, the Governor conducted him to the Brook, and there they embraced each other and he departed.[68]

---

64. Guns.

65. Cheerful; also, pleasing in appearance. See *Oxford English Dictionary*, 3rd ed., s.v. "Lusty," adj. 1a and 2a.

66. Possibly wampum. See note 54 in *Good News*.

67. Probably "murrey," a reddish purple or blood red color. See *Oxford English Dictionary*, 3rd ed., s.v. "Murrey," n.1, 1.

68. A short time later, Emmanuel Altham, who was one of the investors in Plimoth colony and who traveled to New England in 1623, described Massasoit in similar terms: "He is as proper a man as ever was seen in this country, and very courageous. He is very subtle for a savage, and he goes like the rest of his men, all naked but only a black wolf skin he wears upon his shoulder. And about the breadth of a span he wears beads about his middle. And these beads they make themselves, which they account as gold above silver before the beads we bring out of England." See Altham, Emmanuel Altham to Sir Edward Altham, 30.

From William Bradford, *History of the Plimoth Plantation Containing An Account of the Voyage of the 'Mayflower' Written by William Bradford* (London: Ward and Downey, 1896), 80–81.

William Bradford recorded a slightly different version of the agreement between the colonists and the Wampanoags in his history of Plimoth colony. This account omits the colonists' promise to leave their guns behind when they entered the Wampanoags' villages but requires that the Wampanoags leave behind their weapons when at Plimoth.[69]

With whom after friendly entertainment, & some gifts given him,[70] they made a peace with him (which hath now continued this 24 years) In these terms: 1. That neither he nor any of his, should injure or do hurt, to any of their people.

2. That if any of his, did any hurts to any of theirs, he should send the offender, that they might punish him.

3. That if any things were taken away from any of theirs, he should cause it to be restored; and they should do the like to his.

4. If any did unjustly war against him, they would aid him; If any did war against them, he should aid them.

5. He should send to his neighbors confederates, to certify them of this, that they might not wrong them, but might be likewise comprised in the conditions of peace.

6. That when their men came to them, they should leave their bows and arrows behind them.

---

69. On this omission, see Salisbury, *Manitou and Providence*, 115.
70. Massasoit.

Edward Winslow, "A Journey to *Packanokick*, The Habitation
of the Great King Massasoyt. As also our Message, the *Answer
and Entertainment We Had of Him*," in *A Relation Or Journal*
(London, 1622), 40–48.

This selection details Winslow's account of his first journey to Massasoit's village at Sowams, in 1621. Winslow described the Algonquian people he met on this journey and the country in addition to
several events and experiences that surprised him.

It seemed good to the Company for many considerations to send some
amongst them to *Massasoyt*, the greatest Commander amongst the Savages, bordering about us; partly to know where to find them, if occasion
served, as also to see their strength, discover the Country, prevent abuses
in their disorderly coming unto us, make satisfaction for some conceived
injuries to be done on our parts,[71] and to continue the league of Peace and
Friendship between them and us. For these, and the like ends, it pleased
the Governor[72] to make choice of *Steven Hopkins*,[73] & *Edward Winslow*
to go unto him, and having a fit opportunity, by reason of a Savage, called
Tisquantum (that could speak English) coming unto us; with all expedition provided a Horse-mans coat, of red Cotton, and laced with a slight
lace for a present, that both they and their message might be the more acceptable amongst them. The Message was as followeth; That forasmuch
as his subjects came often and without fear, upon all occasions amongst
us, so we were now come unto him, and in witness of the love and good
will the English bear unto him, the Governor hath sent him a coat, desiring that the Peace and Amity that was between them and us might
be continued, not that we feared them, but because we intended not to
injure any, desiring to live peaceably: and as with all men, so especially

71. Winslow is probably referring to the corn that the colonists took from Native
stores shortly after their arrival. Several more references to this corn are noted below.
72. William Bradford had recently been chosen governor.
73. Steven Hopkins may have been a military man, assigned to assist Standish. He
apparently brought his wife and several servants with him to New England; he was not
part of the Separatist community at Leiden. See Young, *Chronicles of the Pilgrim Fathers*,
126–27, n. 2.

with them our nearest neighbors. But whereas his people came very often, and very many together unto us, bringing for the most part their wives and children with them, they were well come; yet we being but strangers as yet at *Patuxet, alias New-Plimoth*, and not knowing how our Corn might prosper, we could no longer give them such entertainment as we had done, and as we desired still to do: yet if he would be pleased to come himself, or any special friend of his desired to see us, coming from him they should be well-come; and to the end we might know them from others, our Governor had sent him a copper Chain, desiring if any Messenger should come from him to us, we might know him by bringing it with him, and hearken and give credit to his Message accordingly. Also requesting him that such as have skins, should bring them to us, and that he would hinder the multitude from oppressing us with them. And whereas at our first arrival at *Paomet* (called by us *Cape Cod*) we found there Corn buried in the ground, and finding no inhabitants but some graves of dead new buried, took the Corn, resolving if ever we could hear of any that had right thereunto, to make satisfaction to the full for it, yet since we understood the owners thereof were fled for fear of us, our desire was either to pay them with the like quantity of corn, English meal, or any other Commodities we had to pleasure them withal; requesting him that some one of his men might signify so much unto them, and we would content him for his pains.[74] And last of all, our Governor requested one favor of him, which was, that he would exchange some of their Corn for feed with us, that we might make trial of which best agreed with the soil where we live.

With these presents and message we set forward the tenth of June, about 9. a clock in the Morning, our guide resolving that night to rest at *Namaschet*,[75] a Town under *Massasoyt*, and conceived by us to be very near, because the Inhabitants flocked so thick upon every slight occasion amongst us: but we found it to be some fifteen English miles. On the way we found some ten or twelve men women and children, which had pestered us, till we were weary of them, perceiving that (as the manner of

---

74. This is the second reference to the theft and repayment of this corn. See also the reference in Winslow's "Letter sent from New England" below.

75. Nemasket, also referred to as Mattapoiset or Mattapuyst. It seems to have been one of the Wampanoag communities that had placed itself under Massasoit's protection. Coubatant (also spelled Combatant) was the sachem there.

them all is) where victual is easiest to be got, there they live, especially in the Summer: by reason whereof our Bay affording many Lobsters, they resort every spring tide thither: & now returned with us to *Namaschet*. Thither we came about 3. a clock after noon the Inhabitants entertaining us with joy, in the best manner they could, giving us a kind of bread called by them *Maizium*, and the spawn of Shads, which then they got in abundance, in so much as they gave us spoons to eat them, with these they boiled musty Acorns, but of the Shads we ate heartily. After this they desired one of our men to shoot at a Crow, complaining what damage they sustained in their Corn by them, who shooting some fourscore off and killing, they much admired it, as other shots on other occasions. After this *Tisquantum* told us we should hardly in one day reach *Packanokick*, moving us to go some 8. miles further, where we should find more store and better victuals than there: Being willing to hasten our Journey we went, and came thither at Sun setting, where we found many of the *Namascheucks* (they so calling the men of *Namaschet*) fishing upon a Weir which they had made on a River which belonged to them, where they caught abundance of Bass. These welcomed us also, gave us of their fish, and we them of our victuals, not doubting but we should have enough where ere we came. There we lodged in the open fields: for houses they had none, though they spent the most of the Summer there. The head of this River is reported to be not far from the place of our abode, upon it are, and have been many Towns, it being a good length. The ground is very good on both sides, it being for the most part cleared: Thousands of men have lived there, which died in a great plague not long since: and pity it was and is to see, so many goodly fields, & so well seated, without men to dress and manure the same. Upon this River dwelleth *Massasoyt*: It cometh into the Sea at the *Narrohiganset* Bay, where the French men so much use. A ship may go many miles up it, as the Savages report, and a shallop to the head of it: but so far as we saw, we are sure a Shallop may.

But to return to our Journey: The next morning we broke our fast, took our leave and departed, being then accompanied with some six Savages, having gone about six miles by the River side, at a known shole place, it being low water, they spoke to us to put off our breeches, for we must wade through. Here let me not forget the valor and courage of some of the Savages, on the opposite side of the river, for there were remaining alive only 2. men, both aged, especially the one being above threescore; These two espying a company of men entering the River, ran very swiftly & low in the grass to meet us at the bank, where with shrill voices and great courage standing charged upon us with their bows, they demanded what we were, supposing us to be enemies, and thinking to take advantage on us in the water: but seeing we were friends, they welcomed us with such food as they had, and we bestowed a small bracelet of Beads on them. Thus far we are sure the Tide ebbs and flows.

Having here again refreshed ourselves we proceeded in our Journey, the weather being very hot for travel, yet the Country so well watered that a man could scarce be dry, but he should have a spring at hand to cool his thirst, beside small Rivers in abundance: But the Savages will not willingly drink, but at a spring head. When we came to any small Brook where no bridge was, two of them desired to carry us through of their own accords, also fearing we were or would be weary, offered to carry our pieces, also if we would lay off any of our clothes, we should have them carried: and as the one of them had found more special kindness from one of the Messengers, and the other Savage from the other so they showed their thankfulness accordingly in affording us all help, and furtherance in the Journey.

As we passed along, we observed that there were few places by the River, but had been inhabited, by reason whereof, much ground was clear, save of weeds which grew higher than our heads. There is much good Timber both Oak, Walnut-tree, Fir, Beech, and exceeding great Chest-nut-trees. The Country in respect of the lying of it, is both Champanie[76] and hilly, like many places in England. In some places its very rocky both above ground and in it: And though the Country be wild and over-grown with woods, yet the trees stand not thick, but a man may well ride a horse amongst them.

Passing on at length, one of the Company an *Indian* espied a man, and told the rest of it, we asked them if they feared any, they told us that if they were *Narrohigganset* men they would not trust them, whereat, we called for our pieces and bid them not to fear; for though they were twenty, we two alone would not care for them: but they hailing him, he

76. Probably a spelling of "champaign," meaning level and open. See *Oxford English Dictionary*, 3rd ed., s.v. "Champaign," adj. 2.

proved a friend, and had only two women with him: their baskets were empty, but they fetched water in their bottles, so that we drank with them and departed. After we met another man with other two women, which had been at Rendezvous by the salt water, and their baskets were full of roasted Crab fishes and the other dried shellfish, of which they gave us, and we ate and drank with them: and gave each of the women a string of Beads, and departed.

After we came to a Town of *Massasoyts*, where we ate Oysters and other fish. From thence we went to *Packanokick*, but *Massasoyt* was not at home, there we stayed, he being sent for: when news was brought of his coming, our guide *Tisquantum* requested that at our meeting, we would discharge our pieces, but one of us going about to charge his piece, the women and children through fear to see him take up his piece, ran away, and could not be pacified, till he laid it down again, who afterward were better informed by our Interpreter.

Massasoyt being come, we discharged our Pieces, and saluted him, who after their manner kindly welcomed us, and took us into his house, and set us down by him, where having delivered our foresaid Message, and Presents, and having put the Coat on his back, and the Chain about his neck, he was not a little proud to behold himself, and his men also to see their King so bravely attired.

For answer to our Message, he told us we were welcome, and he would gladly continue that Peace and Friendship which was between him & us: and for his men they should no more pester us as they had done: Also, that he would send to *Paomet*, and would help us with Corn for seed, according to our request.

This being done, his men gathered near to him, to whom he turned himself, and made a great Speech; they sometime interposing, and as it were, confirming and applauding him in that he said. The meaning whereof was (as far as we could learn) thus: Was not he *Massasoyt* Commander of the Country about them? Was not such a Town his and the people of it? and should they not bring their skins unto us? To which they answered, they were his & would be at peace with us, and bring their skins to us. After this manner, he named at least thirty places, and their answer was as aforesaid to every one: so that as it was delightful, it was tedious unto us.

This being ended, he lighted Tobacco for us, and fell to discoursing of *England*, & of the Kings Majesty, marveling that he would live without a wife. Also he talked of the French-men, bidding us not to suffer them to come to *Narrohiganset,* for it was King JAMES his Country, and he also was King JAMES his man. Late it grew, but victuals he offered none; for indeed he had not any, being he came so newly home. So we desired to go to rest: he laid us on the bed with himself and his wife, they at the one end and we at the other, it being only planks laid a foot from the ground, and a thin Mat upon them. Two more of his chief men for want of room pressed by and upon us; so that we were worse weary of our lodging than of our journey.

The next day being Thursday, many of their Sachims, or petty Governors came to see us, and many of their men also. There they went to their manner of Games for skins and knives. There we challenged them to shoot with them for skins: but they durst not: only they desired to see one of us shoot at a mark, who shooting with Hail-shot they wondered to see the mark so full of holes. About one a clock, *Massasoyt* brought two fishes that he had shot, they were like Bream[77] but three times so big, and better meat. These being boiled there were at least forty looked for share in them, the most ate of them: This meal only we had in two nights and a day, and had not one of us bought a Partridge, we had taken our Journey fasting: Very importunate he was to have us stay with them longer: But we desired to keep the Sabbath at home: and feared we should either be light-headed for want of sleep, for what with bad Lodging, the Savages barbarous singing, (for they use to sing themselves asleep) lice and fleas within doors, and Mosquitoes without, we could hardly sleep all the time of our being there; we much fearing, that if we should stay any longer, we should not be able to recover home for want of strength. So that on the Friday morning before Sun-rising, we took our leave and departed, *Massasoyt* being both grieved and ashamed, that he could no better entertain us: and retaining *Tisquantum* to send from place to place to procure truck for us: and appointing another called *Tokamahamon* in his place, whom we had found faithful before and after upon all occasions.

---

77. A European freshwater fish.

At this town of *Massasoyts*, where we before ate, we were again refreshed with a little fish; and bought about a handful of Meal of their parched Corn, which was very precious at that time of the year, and a small string of dried shell-fish, as big as Oysters. The latter we gave to the six Savages that accompanied us, keeping the Meal for ourselves, when we drank we eat each a spoonful of it with a Pipe of Tobacco, instead of other victuals; and of this also we could not but give them so long as it lasted. Five miles they led us to a house out of the way in hope of victuals: but we found nobody there, and so were but worse able to return home. That night we reached to the weir where we lay before, but the *Namascheucks* were returned: so that we had no hope of anything there. One of the Savages had shot a Shad in the water, and a small Squirrel as big as a Rat, called a *Neuxis*, the one half of either he gave us, and after went to the weir to fish. From hence we wrote to *Plimoth*, and sent *Tokamahamon* before to *Namasket*, willing him from thence to send another, that he might meet us with food at *Namasket*. Two men now only remained with us, and it pleased God to give them good store of fish, so that we were well refreshed. After supper we went to rest, and they to fishing again: more they got and fell to eating a fresh, and retained sufficient ready roast for all our break-fasts. About two a Clock in the morning, arose a great storm of wind, rain, lightning, and thunder, in such violent manner, that we could not keep in our fire; and had the Savages not roasted fish when we were asleep, we had set forward fasting: for the rain still continued with great violence, even the whole day through, till we came within two miles of home.

Being wet and weary, at length we came to *Namaschet*, there we refreshed ourselves, giving gifts to all such as had showed us any kindness. Amongst others one of the six that came with us from *Packanokick* having before this on the way unkindly forsaken us, marveled we gave him nothing, and told us what he had done for us; we also told him of some discourtesies he offered us, whereby he deserved nothing, yet we gave him a small trifle: whereupon he offered us Tobacco: but the house being full of people, we told them he stole some by the way, and if it were of that we would not take it: For we would not receive that which was stolen upon any terms; if we did, our God would be angry with us, and destroy us. This abashed him, and gave the rest great content: but at our departure he would needs carry him on his back through a River, whom he had formerly in some sort abused. Fain they would have had us to lodge there all night: and wondered we would set forth again in such Weather: but GOD be praised, we came safe home that night, though wet, weary, and surbated.

Edward Winslow, "A Letter Sent From *New-England* to a friend in these parts, *setting forth a brief and true Declaration* of the worth of that Plantation; As also certain useful Directions *for such as intend a* Voyage *into those Parts*," in *A Relation Or Journal* (London, 1622), 60–64.

In this letter, Winslow articulated his initial impressions of New England and its people, some of which he would revise in *Good News*. In particular, he later wrote that he had been too optimistic about the ease with which colonists could locate and obtain resources in New England, and he revised his statement that Natives had no religious practices.

Loving, and old Friend, although I received no Letter from you by this Ship, yet forasmuch as I know you expect the performance of my promise, which was, to write unto you truly and faithfully of all things. I have therefore at this time sent unto you accordingly. Referring you for further satisfaction, to our more large Relations. You shall understand, that in this little time, that a few of us have been here, we have built seven dwelling houses, and four for the use of the Plantation, and have made preparation for divers others. We set the last Spring some twenty Acres of *Indian* Corn, and sowed some six Acres of Barley & Peas, and according to the manner of the *Indians,* we manured our ground with Herrings or rather Shads, which we have in great abundance, and take with great ease at our doors. Our Corn did prove well, & God be praised, we had a good increase of *Indian* Corn, and our Barley indifferent good, but our Peas not worth the gathering, for we feared they were too late sown, they came up very well, and blossomed, but the Sun parched them in the blossom; our harvest being gotten in, our Governor sent four men on fowling, that so we might after a more special manner rejoice together, after we had gathered the fruit of our labors; they four in one day killed as much fowl, as with a little help beside, served the Company almost a week, at which time amongst other Recreations, we exercised our Arms, many of the *Indians* coming amongst us, and amongst the rest their greatest King *Massasoyt*, with some ninety men, whom for three days we entertained and feasted, and they went out and killed five Deer, which they brought to the Plantation and bestowed on our Governor, and upon the Captain, and others.[78] And although it be not always so plentiful, as it was at this time with us, yet by the goodness of God, we are so far from want, that we often wish you partakers of our plenty. We have found the *Indians* very faithful in their Covenant of Peace with us; very loving and ready to pleasure us: we often go to them, and they come to us; some of us have been fifty miles by Land in the Country with them, the occasions and Relations whereof you shall understand by our general and more full Declaration of such things as are worth the noting, yea, it hath pleased God so to possess the *Indians* with a fear of us, and love unto us, that not only the greatest King amongst them called *Massasoyt*, but also all the Princes and peoples round about us, have either made suit unto us, or been glad of any occasion to make peace with us, so that seven of them at once have sent their messengers to us to that end, yea an Isle at sea, which we never saw hath also together with the former yielded willingly to be under the protection, and subjects to our sovereign Lord King JAMES, so that there is now great peace amongst the *Indians* themselves, which was not formerly, neither would have been but for us; and we for our parts walk as peaceably and safely in the wood, as in the high-ways in *England*, we entertain them familiarly in our houses, and they as friendly bestowing their Venison on us. They are a people without any Religion, or knowledge of any God,[79] yet very trusty, quick of apprehension, ripe witted, just, the men and women go

---

78. This description is now identified as the first Thanksgiving, although the colonists would have viewed it less as a holiday or a feast and more as a ritual of thanks that could restore order to spiritual and social realms and that acknowledged their safe passage through dangers. See Hall, *Worlds of Wonder*, chap. 4. The Wampanoags may have viewed the event as one among several occasions of hospitality that established and confirmed their relationship with the colonists.

79. In *Good News*, Winslow revised this statement that the Natives have no religion. See note 97 in Part I.

naked, only a skin about their middles; for the temper of the air, here it
agreeth well with that in *England,* and if there be any difference at all, this
is somewhat hotter in Summer, some think it to be colder in Winter, but
I cannot out of experience so say; the air is very clear and not foggy, as
hath been reported. I never in my life remember a more seasonable year,
than we have here enjoyed: and if we have once but Kine,[80] Horses, and
Sheep, I make no question, but men might live as contented here as in any
part of the world. For fish and fowl, we have great abundance, fresh Cod in
the Summer is but course meat with us, our Bay is full of Lobsters all the
Summer, and affordeth variety of other Fish; in September we can take a
Hogshead of Eels in a night, with small labor, & can dig them out of their
beds, all the Winter we have Mussels and Othus[81] at our doors: Oysters
we have none near, but we can have them brought by the *Indians* when
we will; all the Spring time the earth sendeth forth naturally very good
Sallet[82] Herbs: here are Grapes, white and red, and very sweet and strong
also. Strawberries, Gooseberries, Raspas,[83] &c. Plums of three sorts, with
black and red, being almost as good as a Damsen:[84] abundance of Roses,
white, red, and damask: single, but very sweet indeed; the Country wanteth only industrious men to employ, for it would grieve your hearts (if
as I) you had seen so many miles together by goodly Rivers uninhabited,
and withal to consider those parts of the world wherein you live, to be
even greatly burdened with abundance of people. These things I thought
good to let you understand, being the truth of things as near I could
experimentally take knowledge of, and that you might on our behalf give
God thanks who hath dealt so favorably with us.

Our supply of men from you came the ninth of *November* 1621. putting
in at Cape Cod, some eight or ten leagues from us, the *Indians* that dwell
thereabout were they who were owners of the Corn which we found in
Caves, for which we have given them full content, and are in great league
with them, they sent us word there was a ship near unto them, but thought

---

80. Cows.
81. Young suggests this word is an error for "others." See Young, *Chronicles of the Pilgrim Fathers,* 233, n. 5.
82. Probably salad.
83. An obsolete word for raspberries. See *Oxford English Dictionary,* 3rd ed., s.v.
"Raspis," n.2, 1a.
84. A small plum. Spelled inconsistently throughout the seventeenth century; now
spelled damson. See *Oxford English Dictionary,* 1st ed., s.v. "Damson," n., 1a.

it to be a French man, and indeed for our selves, we expected not a friend so soon. But when we perceived that she made for our Bay, the Governor commanded a great Piece to be shot off, to call home such as were abroad at work; whereupon every man, yea, boy that could handle a Gun were ready, with full resolution, that if she were an Enemy, we would stand in our just defense, not fearing them, but God provided better for us then we supposed; these came all in health unto us, not any being sick by the way (otherwise then by Sea sickness) and so continue at this time, by the blessing of God, the good wife *Ford* was delivered of a son the first night she landed, and both of them are very well. When it pleaseth God, we are settled and fitted for the fishing business, and other trading, I doubt not but by the blessing of God, the gain will give content to all; in the mean time, that we have gotten we have sent by this ship, and though it be not much, yet it will witness for us, that we have not been idle, considering the smallness of our number all this Summer. We hope the Merchants will accept of it, and be encouraged to furnish us with things needful for further employment, which will also encourage us to put forth our selves to the uttermost. Now because I expect your coming unto us with other of our friends, whose company we much desire, I thought it good to advertise you of a few things needful; be careful to have a very good bread-room to put your Biscuits in, let your Cask for Beer and Water be Iron-bound for the first tyre[85] if not more; let not your meat be dry salted, none can better do it then the Sailors; let your meal be so hard trod in your Cask that you shall need an Adze or Hatchet to work it out with: Trust not too much on us for Corn at this time, for by reason of this last company that came, depending wholly upon us, we shall have little enough till harvest; be careful to come by some of your meal to spend by the way, it will much refresh you, build your Cabins as open as you can, and bring good store of clothes, and bedding with you; bring every man a Musket or fowling Piece, let your Piece be long in the barrel, and fear not the weight of it, for most of our shooting is from Stands; bring juice of Lemons,[86] and take it

---

85. Possibly tier.

86. It is possible that Winslow suggested that future colonists bring lemon juice to New England to prevent scurvy. Bradford noted that many colonists died from scurvy during their first winter in New England. Travelers were aware that the juice of lemons and oranges cured scurvy, even if they did not know that scurvy was caused by a deficiency of vitamin C. See Lloyd, *British Seaman*, 45–46.

fasting, it is of good use; for hot waters, Anise-seed water is the best, but use it sparingly: if you bring any thing for comfort in the Country, Butter or Sallet oil, or both is very good; our *Indian* Corn even the coursest, maketh as pleasant meat as Rice, therefore spare that unless to spend by the way; bring Paper, and Linced[87] oil for your Windows, with Cotton yarn for your Lamps; let your shot be most for big Fowls, and bring store of Powder and shot: I forbear further to write for the present, hoping to see you by the next return, so I take my leave, commending you to the LORD for a safe conduct unto us. Resting in him
Plimoth in New-England
    this 11. of December.
      1621.

                                 Your Loving Friend
                                   E. W.

From Phenehas Pratt, *A Declaration Of The Affairs Of The English People That First Inhabited New England* (1662).

In this selection, Pratt described the events leading up to the Plimoth colonists' attack on the Massachusetts as well as the attack itself. As Pratt noted, he was too weak to accompany Myles Standish and other Plimoth men to Wessagusset for the attack because he had run to Plimoth to warn the colonists that he believed the Massachusetts were planning to kill them.

[this] morning I see a man going into one of their [the Massachusetts] houses, weary with traveling & Galded[88] on his feet. then I said to Mr. Salsbery, our Chirurgeon,[89] surely their Sachem hath employed him for some intent to make war upon us. Then I took a Bag with gunpowder and put it in my pocket with the Top of the bag hanging out—& went to

---

87. Perhaps linseed.
88. This word has the same meaning as "gall," to "make sore by chafing or rubbing." See *Oxford English Dictionary*, 3rd ed., s.v. "Gall," v.1, 1a.
89. Surgeon.

the house where the man was laid upon a Mat. The woman of the house took hold of the bag saying what is this so big? I said it is good for Savages to eat and struck her on the Arm as hard as I could. Then she said, Matchit powder English men, much Matchit.[90] By and by Abordicis[91] bring Much Men, Much Sannups,[92] & kill you & all English men at We-saguscus & Patuxet. The man that lay upon the mats seeing this was Angry and in a great Rage & the woman seemed to be sore afraid. Then I went out of the house and said to a young man that could best under-stand their Language, go Ask the woman but not in the mans hearing why the man was Angry & she Afraid. Our interpreter Coming to me said, these are the words of the woman, the man will [tell?] Abordicis what I said & he & all Indians will be angry with me [. . .] This Pexworth said, I love you. I said I love you. I said I love you as well as you Love me. Then he said in broken English, me hear you can make the Likeness of men & of women, dogs & deers, in wood & stone. [. . .] I said, I can see a knife in your hand, with an Ill favored face upon the haft[93]—Then he gave it into my hand to see his workmanship & said, this knife cannot see, it Can not hear, it Can not speak, but by & by it can eat. I have Another knife at home with a face upon the haft as like a man as this is like a woman. That knife Can not see, it Can not hear, it Can not speak, but it can eat. It hath killed much French men & by & by this knife & that knife shall marry & you shall be there. The knife at home he had kept for a monument, from the Time they had killed Monsieur Finch. but as the word went out of his mouth, I had a good will to thrust it in his belly—He said I see you are much angry. I said Guns are Longer than knives. Some time after this their Sachem Came suddenly upon us with a great number of Armed men but their spies seeing us in a Readiness he & some of his Chief men turned into one of their houses a quarter of An hour. Then we met them without the pale of our plantation & brought them in. Then said I to a young man that could best speak their Language—Ask Pexworth why they come thus Armed. He Answered, our Sachem is angry with you. I

90. "Matchit" is an Algonquian word for "bad."
91. Pratt may mean to refer to Natives who lived north of Massachusetts Bay. He seems to have been concerned that the Massachusetts and Wampanoags were planning to join with the Abenaki.
92. A married man.
93. Handle.

said, Tell him if he be Angry with us, we be Angry with him. Then said
their Sachem, English men, when you Come into the Country, we gave
you gifts and you gave us gifts, we bought and sold with you and we were
friends, & now tell me if I or any of my men have done you Wrong. We
answered, first tell us if we have done you Any Wrong. He answered,
Some of you steal our Corn & I have sent you word times without number & yet our Corn is stole. I come to see what you will do. We answered,
It is one man which hath done it. Your men have seen us whip him diverse
times besides other manner of punishments & now here he is Bound. We
give him unto you to do with him what you please—He answered, it is
not just dealing. If my men wrong my neighbor sachem or his men he
sends me word & I beat or kill my men, according to the offense. If his
men wrong me or my men, I send him word & he beats or kills his men
According to the offense. All Sachems do Justice by their own men. If not
we say they are all Agreed & then we fight, & now I say you all steal my
Corn. At this Time some of them, seeing some of our men upon our fort,
began to start, saying Machit Pesconk, that is naughty Guns. Then Looking Round about them went a way in a great Rage—At this Time we
strengthened our watch until we had no food left. In these times the Savages oftentimes did Creep upon the snow starting behind Bushes & trees
to see whether we kept watch or not—[. . .] then in the night, going into
our Court of Guard, I see one man dead before me & Another at my right
hand & An other at my left for want [. . .] o all the people in New England
that shall hear of these times of our weak beginnings Consider what was
the strength of the Arm of flesh or the wit of man. Therefore in the times
of your greatest distress put your trust in God. The offender being bound,
we let him loose, because we had no food to give him, Charging him to
gather Ground Nuts[94] Clams & Mussels as other men did & steal no
more—One or two days after this, the savages brought him, leading him
by the arms, saying here is the Corn. Come see the place where he stole
it. Then we kept him bound some few days. After this two of our Company said we have been at the Sachems house & they have near finished
their last Canoe that they may encounter with our ship. Their greatest
Care is how to send their Armies to Plimoth because of the snow. Then

---

94. The underground stem or root of the wild bean; also refers to the plant itself. See
Oxford English Dictionary, 1st ed., s.v. "Ground-nut," n., 1.

we prepared to meet them there.[95] One of our company said they have killed one of our hogs. An other said, one of them struck at me with his knife; & others say they threw dust in our faces. Then said Pexworth to me, give me powder & Guns & I will give you much corn. I said, by & by men bring ships & vittles. But when we understood their plot was to kill all English people in one day when the snow was gone, I would have sent a man to Plimoth, but none were willing to go.[96] Then I said if Plimoth men know not of this Treacherous plot, they & we are all dead men, Therefore if God willing, to morrow I will go. That night a young man wanting wit told Pexworth early in the Morning. Pexworth came to me & said in English, Me hear you go to Patuxet; you will lose your self—the bears and the wolves will eat you, but because I Love you I will send my boy Nahomet with you; & I will give you victuals to eat by the way & to be merry with your friends when you Come there. I said, Who told you so great a Lie that I may kill him. He said, it is no lie, you shall not know. Then he went home to his house—Then Came 5 men[97] Armed. We said Why Come you thus Armed. They said, we are friends, [you] carry Guns where we dwell & we carry bow & Arrows where you dwell. These Attended me 7 or 8 days & nights. Then they supposing it[98] was a lie, were Careless of their watch near two hours on the morning. Then said I to our Company, now is the Time to Run to Plimoth. Is there any Compass to be found. They said, none but them that belong to the ship. I said they are too Big. I have borne no arms of Defense this 7 or 8 days. Now if I take my arms they will mistrust me. Then they said, the savages will pursue after you & kill you & we shall never see you Again. Thus with other words of great Lamentation we parted. Then I took a hoe & went to the Long Swamp near by their houses & dug on the edge thereof as if I had been looking for ground nuts but seeing no man I went in & Run through it. Then Looking Round a bout me, I Run Southward till 3 of the Clock, but the snow being in many places, I was the more distressed because of my foot steps.[99] The sun being beclouded I wandered not knowing my

95. That is, to meet the Massachusetts at Plimoth.
96. Here Pratt seems to be acting in the place of John Sanders, the leader of the men at Wessagusset.
97. Massachusett men.
98. The report that Pratt planned to go to Plimoth.
99. That is, his fear that the Massachusetts would be able to track him.

way; but at the Going down of the sun, it appeared Red, then hearing a great howling of wolves I came to a River, The water being deep & cold & many Rocks, I passed through with much Ado. Then was I in great distress, faint for want of food, weary with Running, fearing to make a fire because of them that pursued me. Then I came to a deep dell or hole, there being much wood fallen into it. Then I said in my thoughts, this is Gods providence that here I may make a fire. Then having made a fire, the stars began to appear—and I saw Ursa Major [...]. The day following I began to travel [...] but being unable I went back to the fire [...] & about 3 of the clock I came to that part [...] Plimoth bay where there is a Town of Later Time [called?] Duxbery. Then passing by the water on my left hand [I?] came to a brook & there was a path. Having but a short Time to Consider & fearing to go beyond the plantation I kept Running in the path, then passing through James River I said in my thoughts, now am I as a deer Chased [by?] the wolves. If I perish what will be the Condition of distressed English men. Then finding a piece of a [...] I took it up & Carried it in my hand. Then finding a [...] Jerkin,[100] I Carried them under my arm. Then said I [...] God hath given me these two tokens for my Comfort, that now he will give me my life for a prayer. Then Running down a hill [I saw?] an English man Coming in the path before me. Then I sat down on a tree & Rising up to salute him said, Mr. Hamdin[101] I am Glad to see you alive. He said I am Glad & full of wonder to see you alive, let us sit down I see you are weary. I said, Let [...] eat some parched corn. Then he said, I know the Cause why [you?] Come: Massasoit hath sent word to the Governor to let him [know?] that Aberdikees & his Confederates have contrived a plot [...]. Stay & we will go with you. The next day a young [...] named Hugh Stacye went forth to fell a tree & see two [men?] rising from the Ground. They said Aberdikees had sent [...] the Governor that he might send men to truck for much Beaver but they would not go, but said, Was not there An English [...] Come from Wesaguscus. He Answered he came [...] They said he was their friend, and said come and see [...] But they Turned another way. [...] Providence to

---

100. A jacket.
101. Probably John Hamden, the man who traveled to Massasoit's sick bed with Winslow.

us was great in those times as appeareth [...] after the time of the Arrival of the first ship [...] Massasoit Came to Plimoth & there made a [...] peace, for an Indian Called Tisquantum Came to them & speak English. They Asked him how he learned to speak English? He said that An Englishman Called Capt Hunt Came into the Harbor pretending to trade for beaver & stole 24 men & their beaver & Carried & Sold them in Spain & from thence with much ado he went into England & from England with much ado he got into his own Country—This man told Massasoit what wonders he had seen in England & that if he Could make English his friends then [...] Enemies that were too strong from him would be Constrained to bow to him [...] Two or 3 days after my Coming to Plimoth, 10 or 11 men went in a boat to our plantation, but I being faint was not able to go with them. They first gave warning to the master of the ship & Then Contrived how to make sure of the Lives of two of their Chief men, Wituwamet of whom they boasted no Gun would kill, and Pexworth a subtle man. These being slain they fell upon others where they could find them. Then Abordikees hearing that some of his men were killed Came to try his manhood, but as they were starting behind bushes & trees, one of them was shot in the Arm. At this time An Indian called Hobbamock that formerly had fled for his life from his Sachem to Plimoth approved himself a valiant man, in fighting & pursuing after them.[102] Two of our men were killed that they took in their houses at An Advantage—this Time [...] were instruments in the [...] hands of God for [...] their own lives and ours. They took the head of [Wituwamet] & set it on their fort at Plimoth.

---

102. This account of Hobbamock and Massasoit contradicts Winslow's description of Hobbamock as loyal to and trusted by Massasoit.

John Robinson to William Bradford, 1623, in *History of the Plimoth Plantation Containing An Account of the Voyage of the 'Mayflower' Written by William Bradford* (London: Ward and Downey, 1896), 113–14.

John Robinson was ordained as a clergyman in the Church of England in the 1590s, but he began to speak out against the church in 1603. He resigned his position as a fellow at Corpus Christi College, Cambridge, in 1604, and he joined a Separatist congregation in Scrooby as one of its leaders. In 1608, he traveled to Amsterdam and then to Leiden to escape persecution. Robinson supported the migration of members of his congregation to America, but he never traveled to New England himself. This letter was written in response to Bradford's message regarding the colonists' attack on the Massachusetts. Winslow probably carried it to Plimoth when he returned to New England in March 1624.

Robinson to M Bradford

My loving & much beloved friend, whom God hath hitherto preserved, preserve, and keep you still to his glory, and the good of many; that his blessing may make your godly, and wise endeavors answerable to the valuation which they there have, & set upon the same. Of your love to, and care for us here we never doubted, so are we glad to take knowledge of it, in that fullness we do, our love & care to, and for you, is mutual, though our hopes of coming unto you be small, and weaker than ever. But of this at large in M Brewsters letter with whom you, and he with you mutually I know communicate your letters, as I desire you may do these.

Concerning the killing of those poor Indians, of which we heard at first by reports and since by more certain relation, oh how happy a thing had it been, if you had converted some, before you had killed any, besides where blood is once begun to be shed; it is seldom stanched of a long time after. You will say they deserved it, I grant it, but upon what provocations, and invitments,[103] by those heathenish Christians.[104] Besides you being

---

103. Invitations.

104. Robinson is probably referring to the colonists at Wessagusset.

no magistrates over them, were to consider, not what they deserved, but what you were by necessity constrained to inflict. Necessity of this especially of killing so many (and many more it seems they would, if they could) I see not. Methinks, one or two principals should have been full enough, according to that approved rule, the punishments to a few, and the fear to many. Upon this occasion, let me be bold to exhort you, seriously to consider of the disposition of your captain,[105] whom I love, and am persuaded, the Lord in greatest mercy and for much good, hath sent you him, if you use him aright. He is a man humble, and meek amongst you, and towards all in ordinary course. But now if this be merely from an humane spirit, there is cause to fear that by occasion, especially of provocation, there may be wanting that tenderness of the life of man (made after gods Image) which is meet. It is also a thing more glorious, in mens eyes than pleasing in gods, or convenient for Christians, to be a terror to poor barbarous people; and indeed I am afraid lest by these occasions, others should be drawn to affect a kind of ruffling course in the world. I doubt not but you will take in good part these things which I write, and as there is cause make use of them. It were to us more comfortable, and convenient, that we communicated our mutual helps in presence; but seeing that cannot be done, we shall always long after you, and love you, and wait to gods appointed time. The adventurers it seems have neither money, nor any great mind of us, for the most part, they deny it, to be any part of the covenants betwixt us, that they should transport us, neither do I look for any further help from them, till means come from you. We here are strangers in effect to the whole course, and so both we, and you (save as your own wisdoms, and worths, have interested you further) of principals intended in this business are scarce accessories. My wife with me, resalutes you & yours unto him who is the same to his in all places, and near to them, which are far, from one an other, I commend you and all with you, resting

    Yours truly loving
    John Robinson
Leyden, Dec 19, 1623

---

105. Myles Standish.

Bibliography

Primary Sources

Acosta, José de. *The Natural and Moral History of the East and West Indies . . . Written in Spanish by Joseph Acosta and translated into English by E.G.* Trans. E.G. London, 1604.

Altham, Emmanuel. Emmanuel Altham to Sir Edward Altham, September 1623. In *Three Visitors to Early Plymouth*, edited by Sydney V. James Jr., 23–35. Bedford, Mass.: Applewood Books, 1997.

Apess, William. "Eulogy on King Philip." In *A Son of the Forest and Other Writings*, edited by Barry O'Connell, 105–38. Amherst: University of Massachusetts Press, 1997.

Arber, Edward. *The Story of the Pilgrim Fathers, 1606–1623, AD; as told by Themselves, their Friends, and their Enemies.* London: Ward & Downey, 1897.

Bainbridge, John. *An Astronomical Description of the late Comet from the 18. Of Novemb. 1618 to the 16. of December following.* London, 1619.

Bradford, William. *History of the Plimoth Plantation Containing An Account of the Voyage of the 'Mayflower' Written by William Bradford.* London: Ward and Downey, 1896.

———. *Of Plymouth Plantation 1620–1647, by William Bradford*, edited by Samuel Eliot Morison. New York: Alfred A. Knopf, 1952.

Bradford, William, and Edward Winslow. "From Mourt's Relation." In vol. A of *The Norton Anthology of American Literature*, edited by Wayne Franklin, 71–75. 8th ed. New York: Norton, 2011.

A brief Relation of the Discovery And Plantation Of New England . . . and the division of the whole Territory into Counties, Baronries, &c. London, 1622.

Champlain, Samuel de. Vol. 1 of *The Works of Samuel de Champlain, 1599–1607*, edited and translated by H. H. Langton and W. F. Ganong. Toronto: The Champlain Society, 1922.

Cushman, Robert. *A Sermon Preached at Plimoth in New England . . . Written in the year 1621.* London, 1621.

Dermer, Thomas. "To his Worshipful Friend M. Samuel Purchas, Preacher of the Word, at the Church a Little within *Ludgate, London.*" In *Purchas His Pilgrims, in Five Books . . . The Fourth Part,* edited by Samuel Purchas, 1778–79. London, 1625.

Eliot, John. *Tears of Repentance: Or, A Further Narrative of the Progress of the Gospel Amongst the Indians In New-England . . . Published by the corporation for propagating the Gospel there, for the satisfaction and comfort of such as wish well thereunto.* London, 1653.

The Glorious Progress of the Gospel, Amongst the Indians in New England . . . together with an appendix to the foregoing letters, holding forth conjectures, observations, and applications, by J.D. London, 1649.

Gorges, Ferdinando. "A Description of New England." In *America, Painted to the Life . . . More especially, an absolute Narrative of the North parts of America, and of the Discoveries and Plantations of our English in Virginia, New England, and Barbados.* London, 1659.

———. *A Briefe Narration of the Originall Undertakings of the Advancement of Plantations Into the Parts of America . . . Written by the right Worshipful, Sir Ferdinando Gorges Knight and Governour of the Fort and Island of Plymouth in Devonshire.* London, 1658.

Hamor, Ralph. *A true discourse of the present estate of Virginia and the success of the affairs there till the 18 of June. 1614 . . . Written by Ralph Hamor the younger, late secretary in that colony.* London, 1615.

Harcourt, Robert. *A Relation of a Voyage to Guiana, Describing the Climate, Situation, Fertilitie, Provisions and Commodities of that Country . . . together with the manners, customs, behaviours, and dispositions of the people.* London, 1613.

Harriot, Thomas. *A Brief and True Report of the New Found Land of Virginia . . . By Thomas Harriot, servant to the above named Sir Walter, a member of the Colony, and there employed in discovering.* Frankfurt, 1590.

The Holy Bible Containing the Old Testament and the New. Translated into the Indian Language. Cambridge, 1663.

Jameson, J. Franklin, ed. *Narratives of New Netherland, 1609–1664.* New York: Charles Scribner's Sons, 1909.

Lane, Ralph. "An Account of the Particularities of the Imployments of the *English Men Left in Virginia by Sir Richard Greenevill Under the Charge of Master Ralfe Lane General of the Same, From the 17. of August,* 1585, until the 18. of June 1586, At Which Time They Departed the Country: Sent, and Directed to Sir Walter Ralegh." In *Principal Navigations, Voyages and Discoveries of the English Nation,* edited by Richard Hakluyt, 737–47. London, 1589.

Lery, John de. *History of a Voyage to the Land of Brazil*. Translated by Janet Whatley. Berkeley: University of California Press, 1993.

Mather, Increase. *A Relation of the Troubles which have happened in New-England . . . Together with a Historical Discourse concerning the Prevalency of Prayer shewing that New Englands late deliverance from the Rage of the Heathen is an eminent Answer of Prayer*. Boston, 1677.

Morton, Thomas. "Manners and Customs of the Indians." In *Old South Leaflets*, no. 87. Boston: 1899.

———. *New English Canaan or New Canaan. Containing an Abstract of New England, Composed in three Bookes . . . written by Thomas Morton*. Amsterdam, 1637.

Oviedo y Valdés, Gonzalo Fernández de. "The History of the West Indies." In *The Decades of the New World or West India . . . Written in the Latine Tongue by Peter Martyr of Angleria, and Translated into English by Richard Eden*, 173–214. London, 1555.

Pory, John. John Pory to the Earl of Southhampton, 13 January 1622/23. In *Three Visitors to Early Plymouth*, edited by Sydney V. James Jr., 4–8. Bedford, Mass.: Applewood Books, 1997.

———. John Pory to the Governor of Virginia, Autumn 1622. In *Three Visitors to Early Plymouth*, edited by Sydney V. James Jr., 14–18. Bedford, Mass.: Applewood Books, 1997.

Pratt, Phenehas. *A Declaration of the Affairs of the English People that First Inhabited New England*. 1662. Manuscript. Commonwealth of Massachusetts State Archives. Boston.

———. *A Declaration of the Affairs of the English People that First Inhabited New England*, edited by Richard Frothingham. Boston: Press of TR Marvin & Son, 1858.

Purchas, Samuel. Vol. 4 of *Purchas His Pilgrims in five books . . . The fifth, navigations, voyages, traffiques, discoveries, of the English nation in the eastern parts of the world*. London, 1625.

A Relation or Journal of the Beginning and Proceedings of the English Plantation Settled at Plimoth in New England, by Certain English Adventurers both Merchants and Others . . . With an answer to all such objections as are in any way made against the lawfulness of English plantations in those parts. London, 1622.

Rosier, James. *A True Relation of the most prosperous voyage made this present year 1605, by Captaine George Waymouth, in the discovery of the land of Virginia*. London, 1605.

Shepard, Thomas. *The Clear Sun-shine of the Gospel Breaking Forth Upon the Indians in New England . . . Framing Their Hearts to an Earnest Inquirie after the Knowledge of God the Father, and of Jesus Christ the Saviour of the World.* London, 1648.

Smith, John. *A Description of New England: Or, the Observations, and discoveries of Captain* John Smith *(Admiral of that Country) in the North of America, in the year of our Lord 1614 . . . whither this present year, 1616, eight voluntary Ships are gone to make further trial.* London, 1616.

——. *General History of Virginia, New-England, and the Summer Isles with the names of the adventurers, planters, and governors from their first beginning . . . By Captain John Smith sometimes governor in those countries & admiral of New England.* London, 1624.

——. *General History of Virginia, New-England, and the Summer Isles with the names of the adventurers, planters, and governors from their first beginning . . . By Captain John Smith sometimes governor in those countries & admiral of New England.* London, 1632.

Winthrop, John. *Journal of John Winthrop, 1630–1649,* edited by Richard S. Dunn, James Savage, and Laetitia Yaendle. Cambridge: The Belknap Press of Harvard University Press, 1996.

Vespucci, Amerigo. *The Letters of Amerigo Vespucci.* Translated by Clements R. Markham. London: Hakluyt Society, 1894.

Williams, Roger. *A Key into the Language of America.* London, 1643.

Winslow, Edward. *Good News From New England: Or, A True Relation of Things Very Remarkable at the Plantation of* Plimoth *in New-England. Shewing the Wondrous Providence and Goodness of God, in their Preservation and Continuance,* Being Delivered from many Apparent Deaths and Dangers. *Together with a Relation of such Religious and Civil Lawes and Customs, as Are in Practice amongst the* Indians, *Adjoyning Them at this day.* As also What Commodities are There to be Raised for the Maintenance of That and Other Plantations in the Said Country. London, 1624.

——. *Good News from New England (excerpt): The Religion and Customs of the Indians Near New Plymouth.* In vol. II: Prose of *The Broadview Anthology of Seventeenth-Century Verse & Prose,* edited by Alan Rudrum, Joseph Black, and Holly Faith Nelson, 236–41. Ontario: Broadview Press, 2001.

Wroth, Lawrence C., ed. *The Voyages of Giovanni da Verrazzano, 1524–1528.* New Haven: Yale University Press, 1970.

Young, Alexander. *Chronicles of the Pilgrim Fathers of the Colony of Plymouth, from 1602 to 1625. Now first collected from original records and contemporaneous printed documents, and illustrated with notes.* Boston: Charles C. Little and James Brown, 1841.

Secondary Sources

Allen, Paula Gunn. *Pocahontas: Medicine Woman, Spy, Entrepreneur, Diplomat.* New York: Harper Collins, 2004.

Bailyn, Bernard. *The New England Merchants in the Seventeenth Century.* Cambridge: Harvard University Press, 1979.

Bangs, Jeremy Dupertuis. *Pilgrim Edward Winslow: New England's First International Diplomat.* Boston: New England Historic Genealogical Society, 2004.

Bragdon, Kathleen J. *Native People of Southern New England, 1500–1650.* Norman: University of Oklahoma Press, 1996.

Bremer, Francis J. "Endecott, John (d. 1665)." In *Oxford Dictionary of National Biography,* online ed., edited by Lawrence Goldman. Oxford: Oxford University Press. www.oxforddnb.com.

Brooks, Lisa. *The Common Pot: The Recovery of Native Space in the Northeast.* Minneapolis: Minnesota University Press, 2008.

Bross, Kristina. *Dry Bones and Indian Sermons: Praying Indians in Colonial America.* Ithaca: Cornell University Press, 2004.

Brown, Matthew P. *The Pilgrim and the Bee: Reading Rituals and Book Culture in Early New England.* Philadelphia: University of Pennsylvania Press, 2007.

Burgess, Walter H. *John Robinson, Pastor of the Pilgrim Fathers: A Study of His Life and Times.* New York: Harcourt, Brace, and Howe, 1920.

Canny, Nicholas P. "The Ideology of English Colonization: From Ireland to America." *William and Mary Quarterly* 3d. ser., 30, no. 4 (1973): 575–98.

Chaplin, Joyce E. "Natural Philosophy and an Early Racial Idiom in North America: Comparing English and Indian Bodies." *William and Mary Quarterly* 3d ser., 54, no. 1 (1997): 229–52.

Cheshire, Neil, Tony Waldron, Alison Quinn, and David Quinn. "Frobisher's Eskimos in England." *Archivaria* 10 (1980): 23–35.

Cheyfitz, Eric. *The Poetics of Imperialism: Translation and Colonization from The Tempest to Tarzan.* 2nd ed. Philadelphia: University of Pennsylvania Press, 1997.

Clark, Charles E. "Gorges, Sir Ferdinando (1568–1647)." In *Oxford Dictionary of National Biography,* online ed., edited by Lawrence Goldman. Oxford: Oxford University Press. www.oxforddnb.com.

Clark, Michael P. Introduction to *The Eliot Tracts. With Letters from John Eliot* to *Thomas Thorowgood and Richard Baxter,* edited by Michael P. Clark, 1–52. Westport, CT: Praeger, 2003.

Cohen, Matt. *The Networked Wilderness: Communicating in Early New England.* Minneapolis: University of Minnesota Press, 2009.

The Controversy on the Comets of 1618: Galileo Galilei, Horatio Grassi, Mario Guiducci, Johann Kepler. Translated by Stillman Drake and C. D. O'Malley. Philadelphia: University of Pennsylvania Press, 1960.

Cook, S. F. "The Significance of Disease in the Extinction of the New England Indians." In Vol. 26 of *Biological Consequences of the European Expansion, 1450–1800,* edited by Kenneth F. Kiple and Stephen V. Beck, 251–74. Burlington: Ashgate, 1997.

Crosby, Alfred W. "Virgin Soil Epidemics as a Factor in the Aboriginal Depopulation in America." *William and Mary Quarterly* 3d ser., 33, no. 2 (1976): 289–99.

Dempsey, Jack. Introduction to *Good News from New England and Other Writings on the Killings at Weymouth Colony,* edited by Jack Dempsey, xvii–lxxiii. Stoneham, Mass.: Jack Dempsey, 2001.

Donohue, Betty Booth. *Bradford's Indian Book: Being the True Roote & Rise of American Letters as Revealed by the Native Text Embedded in* Of Plimoth Plantation. Gainesville: University Press of Florida, 2011.

Egan, James. *Authorizing Experience: Refigurations of the Body Politic in Seventeenth-Century New England Writing.* Princeton: Princeton University Press, 1999.

Field, Jonathan Beecher. *Errands into the Metropolis: New England Dissidents in Revolutionary London.* Lebanon, NH: Dartmouth College Press, 2009.

Finch, Martha L. *Dissenting Bodies: Corporealities in Early New England.* New York: Cornell University Press, 2010.

Fuller, Mary. *Voyages in Print: English Travel to America, 1576–1624.* Cambridge: Cambridge University Press, 1995.

Goddard, Ives. "The Use of Pidgins and Jargons on the East Coast of North America." In *The Language Encounter in the Americas, 1492–1800,* edited by Edward G. Gray and Norman Fiering, 61–78. New York: Berghahn Books, 2000.

Goddard, Ives, and Kathleen J. Bragdon. *Native Writings in Massachusett.* Philadelphia: American Philosophical Society, 1988.

Gragg, Larry. "Vines, Richard (1597/8–1651)." In Oxford Dictionary of National Biography, online ed., edited by Lawrence Goldman. Oxford: Oxford University Press. www.oxforddnb.com.

Hall, David D. *Worlds of Wonder, Days of Judgment: Popular Religious Belief in Early New England.* Cambridge: Harvard University Press, 1990.

Hodge, Frederick Webb. Part I of *Handbook of American Indians North of Mexico*. Washington: Government Printing Office, 1907.

Hoornbeek, Billee. "An Investigation into the Cause or Causes of the Epidemic Which Decimated the Indian Population of New England, 1616–1619." *New Hampshire Archaeologist* 19 (1976–77): 35–46.

Householder, Michael. *Inventing Americans in the Age of Discovery: Narratives of Encounter*. Burlington: Ashgate, 2012.

Huden, John C. *Indian Place Names of New England*. New York: Museum of the American Indian, 1962.

Hulme, Peter. *Colonial Encounters: Europe and the Native Caribbean, 1492–1797*. London: Methuen, 1986.

Jehlen, Myra. "History Before the Fact; or, Captain John Smith's Unfinished Symphony." *Critical Inquiry* 19 (1993): 677–92.

Jones, David S. *Rationalizing Epidemics: Meanings and Uses of American Indian Mortality since 1600*. Cambridge: Harvard University Press, 2004.

Kelton, Paul T. *Epidemics and Enslavement: Biological Catastrophe in the Native Southeast*. Lincoln: University of Nebraska Press, 2007.

Kupperman, Karen Ordahl. "Fear of Hot Climates in the Anglo-American Colonial Experience." *William and Mary Quarterly* 3d. ser., 41, no. 2 (1984): 213–40.

———. *Indians and English: Facing Off in Early America*. Ithaca: Cornell University Press, 2000.

———. "The Puzzle of the American Climate in the Early Colonial Period." *The American Historical Review* 87, no. 5 (1982): 1262–89.

Lewis, Alonzo. *The History of Lynn including Nahant*. Boston, 1844.

Lloyd, Christopher. *The British Seaman, 1200–1860: A Social Survey*. Cranbury, NJ: Associated University Presses, 1970.

Morgan, Edmund S. *Visible Saints: The History of a Puritan Idea*. New York: New York University Press, 1963.

Murray, David. *Indian Giving: Economies of Power in Indian-White Exchanges*. Amherst: University of Massachusetts Press, 2000.

Pagden, Anthony. *European Encounters with the New World*. New Haven: Yale University Press 1993.

———. *The Fall of Natural Man: The American Indian and the Origins of Comparative Ethnology*. Cambridge: Cambridge University Press, 1986.

Parker, Arthur C. *The Constitution of the Five Nations or The Iroquois Book of the Great Law*. Albany: New York State Museum Bulletin, 1916.

Pulsipher, Jenny Hale. "'Subjects . . . Unto the Same King': New England Indians and the Use of Royal Political Power." *Massachusetts Historical Review* 5 (2003): 29–57.

Quinn, David Beers. *The Elizabethans and the Irish*. Ithaca: Cornell University Press, 1966.

Richter, Daniel K. "Tsenacommacah and the Atlantic World." In *The Atlantic World and Virginia, 1550–1624*, edited by Peter C. Mancall, 29–65. Chapel Hill: University of North Carolina Press, 2007.

Rivett, Sarah. *The Science of the Soul in Colonial New England*. Chapel Hill: University of North Carolina Press, 2011.

Robinson, Paul A., Marc A. Kelley, and Patricia E. Rubertone. "Preliminary Biocultural Interpretations from a Seventeenth-Century Narragansett Indian Cemetery in Rhode Island." In *Cultures in Contact: The Impact of European Contacts on Native American Cultural Institutions, A.D. 1000–1800*, edited by William W. Fitzhugh, 107–30. Washington, DC: Smithsonian Institution Press, 1985.

Rostenberg, Leona. "The New World: John Bellamy, 'Pilgrim' Publisher of London." In vol. 1 of Rostenberg's *Literary, Political, Scientific, Religious & Legal Publishing, Printing & Bookselling in England, 1551–1700: Twelve Studies*. New York: Burt Franklin, 1965.

Russell, Conrad. "Hampden, John (1595–1643)." In *Oxford Dictionary of National Biography*, edited by H. C. G. Matthew and Brian Harrison. Oxford: Oxford University Press, 2004. Online ed., edited by Lawrence Goldman, January 2008. www.oxforddnb.com.

Salisbury, Neal. *Manitou and Providence: Indians, Europeans, and the Making of New England, 1500–1643*. New York: Oxford University Press, 1982.

Seeman, Erik. *Death in the New World: Cross-Cultural Encounters, 1492–1800*. Philadelphia: University of Pennsylvania Press, 2010.

Silverman, David. *Faith and Boundaries: Colonists, Christianity, and Community among the Wampanoag Indians of Martha's Vineyard, 1600–1871*. Cambridge: Cambridge University Press, 2005.

Simmons, William Scranton. *Cautantowwit's House: An Indian Burial Ground on the Island of Conanicut in Narragansett Bay*. Providence: Brown University Press, 1970.

Starna, William A. "The Biological Encounter: Disease and the Ideological Domain." *American Indian Quarterly* 16, no. 4 (1992): 511–19.

Travers, Len. "Winslow, Edward (1595–1655)." In *Oxford Dictionary of National Biography*, edited by H. C. G. Matthew and Brian Harrison. Oxford: Oxford University Press, 2004. Online ed., edited by Lawrence Goldman, October 2006. www.oxforddnb.com.

Vaughan, Alden T. *Transatlantic Encounters: American Indians in Britain, 1500–1776*. Cambridge: Cambridge University Press, 2006.

Walsham, Alexandra. *Providence in Early Modern England*. Oxford: Oxford University Press, 1999.

Weaver, Jace. "The Red Atlantic: Transoceanic Cultural Exchanges." *The American Indian Quarterly* 35, no. 3 (2011): 418–63.

White, Ed. "Invisible Tagkanysough." *PMLA* 120, no. 3 (2005): 751–67.

Whitehead, Neil L. "The *Discoverie* as enchanted text." In *The Discoverie of the Large, Rich and Bewtiful Empyre of Guiana*, edited by Neil L. Whitehead, 8–59. Manchester: Manchester University Press, 1997.

———. "The *Discoverie* as ethnological text." In *The Discoverie of the Large, Rich and Bewtiful Empyre of Guiana*, edited by Neil L. Whitehead, 60–116. Manchester: Manchester University Press, 1997.

Wisecup, Kelly. *Medical Encounters: Knowledge and Identity in Early American Literatures*. Amherst: University of Massachusetts Press, 2013.

Wolkins, George G. "Edward Winslow (O.V. 1606–11): King's Scholar and Printer." *Proceedings of the American Antiquarian Society at the Annual Meeting Held in Worcester* 60, no. 2 (18 Oct. 1950): 235–66.

Index

Harriot, Thomas, 6–8, 22
Hobbamock (deity), 103–5
Hobbamock (Wampanoag man): and
Massachusetts' plot, 61, 84, 87, 94–97;
as pniese, 2, 26, 61–62, 76, 94–96; and
relation to Massasoit, 26, 63–65, 80, 163,
163n102; as translator, 3–4, 59n9, 63, 66,
75, 79–81, 83, 86, 94–95, 100, 143
Hobson, Nicholas, 23, 127
Hunt, Thomas, 22–25, 127, 143, 163

Iyanough (Massachusett sachem), 72n46, 98

James I, 38, 144–45, 152, 155
justice: colonial practices of, 73–74, 76, 91,
153–54, 160; Native practices of, 41–42,
65, 75–76, 109–10, 160

Kiehtan, 11, 28, 103–4, 103n97, 106
King Philip's War, 14, 17, 44, 47

Lane, Ralph, 7–8, 110n104
Leiden, 5, 18, 32, 139, 164–65. See also
Separatists

Massachusetts: alleged plot of, 4–5, 34, 36,
39–43, 62, 77–78, 84–87, 90–94, 96–98,
158–61; descriptions of ships by, 130, 133;
illnesses of, 27–29, 72, 98, 129, 132–34,
138–39; relations with Wessagusset, 35,
41–42, 88, 128–30, 158–63; response to
Plimoth's attack, 4, 44, 95–98; trade with
Europeans, 20, 26, 61–63, 72, 93, 137–38;
women of, 95, 97, 159. See also captives:
Massachusetts; Pratt, Phenehas
Massasoit: English descriptions of, 80,
145, 145n68; gifts for, 4, 37–38, 144,
148, 151; illness of, 1–4, 79–84; and the
Massachusetts' plot, 4, 36, 40–41, 44,
84–86, 162; and missionaries, 46–47; as
sachem, 29, 37–38, 64, 80, 107, 144, 147,
151, 155; speeches of, 84, 151
medical practices: of colonists, 3–5, 10, 69,
81–84; as metaphor, 140–41; of Natives,
1–3, 10, 28–29, 79, 81–82, 103, 105–6,
108, 133
Morton, Thomas: and contact-era
epidemics, 135n30, 137–39; and the
Massachusetts, 40, 42; and Plimoth,
15–16, 43, 138–39

Mourt's Relation, 14, 16, 23, 38, 43

Narragansetts: and bundle of arrows, 39,
59–60; and epidemics, 27–29, 37–38, 106,
133; and relations with Europeans, 17, 20,
37, 62–63, 80n65, 116, 150; threats from, 5,
58–59; use of rumors by, 40–41
New England: climate of, 7, 32–34, 35, 102,
112, 156; English missions in, 27–29,
44–47, 141; European descriptions of, 19,
112–16, 123–24, 131–32, 137, 149–50, 156;
exploration of, 6–7, 26–27, 70–71, 121–23,
127, 147–54; resources of, 23, 67–68, 124,
131–32. See also food
New England Algonquians: burial practices
of, 36, 42–43, 108–9, 139; clothing of, 110,
145, 155–56; and colonial encounters, 121–
26, 129–30, 132; European descriptions
of, 122–23, 125–26, 131–32, 145, 155–56;
games, 75, 152; gender relations, 81, 109–
10; greetings, 74–75; language of, 5, 10–11,
47–48, 111, 126, 138, 159; meteorological
knowledge of, 110–11; records of, 111;
religious practices of, 11, 45–47, 87, 102–6,
155; use of rumors, 39–41

Obtakiest (Massachusett sachem), 40, 90,
97. See also Chickataubut
Ousemequin. See Massasoit

Patuxet, 2, 18n54, 22, 27, 37, 64, 82, 86, 92, 97,
139, 143, 148, 159, 161
Pecksuot: death of, 94, 97, 163; and
Phenehas Pratt, 129, 159, 161
Pequots, 44, 47, 133
Pexworth. See Pecksuot
Pilgrims, 14–15. See also Plimoth colonists;
Separatists
plain style, 56–58, 102
Plimoth colonists: and attack on
Massachusetts, 4–5, 9, 12–15, 17, 34–36,
40–44, 90–91, 93–96, 163–65; common
course of labor of, 98–99; and conversion
of Natives, 12, 33–35, 55, 57, 62, 87, 141,
164; day of prayer, 100–101; disruption
of graves by, 42–43, 148; and fears of
conspiracy, 5, 25–26, 39–41, 55, 61–65,
77–78, 84, 86–87, 97–98; and feast day,
154–55; fortifications of, 37, 40, 55–56,
61, 68, 70, 92–93; guns of, 40, 63, 79,

80n65, 86, 145–46, 150–51, 157; illnesses of, 29, 32–33, 47–48, 70, 89, 112, 128, 157; and investors, 5, 18–19, 25, 55–57, 134, 140, 145n64, 157, 165; and theft of corn, 35–36, 42–43, 147–48, 156; and trade with Natives, 5, 26, 37, 61–62, 65, 70–78, 93, 113, 143–44. *See also* Separatists; Wampanoags: alliance with Plimoth

pnieses: and non-human beings, 105–6; and sachems, 2, 26, 29, 84, 106, 108; training of, 106–7. *See also names of individual pnieses*

powahs: and contact-era epidemics, 28–29, 133; as medical and religious practitioners, 1–2, 75, 105–6; and response to colonists, 37, 97

Powhatans, 12, 15, 112, 117n113, 131

Pratt, Phenehas: and journey to Plimoth, 91–92, 161–63; and the Massachusetts, 40–41, 158–60, 162; and Pexsouth, 129–30, 159–61; and Plimoth's attack, 163. *See also* Wessagusset colonists

Prince, Thomas, 15

Providence, 14, 53, 55, 62, 69–70, 77, 92, 102, 114, 162; tale of, 9

Purchas, Samuel, 6, 14, 124, 135

Quadequina, 143–44

Ralegh, Walter, 7, 22
Robinson, John, 34–35, 48, 57n3, 164–65
Rosier, James, 22, 124–26, 134n28

sachems, 2, 28–29, 38, 42, 107–10, 160. *See also names of individual sachems*
Samoset, 37, 143
Sanders, John, 42, 88–91, 93
self-love, 33, 99, 140–42
Separatists: in Leiden, 13n38, 18, 32–33, 139–40; religious beliefs of, 17; views of body of, 32–33. *See also* Plimoth colonists
Slanie, John, 25, 143
Smith, John, 6–7, 14, 26, 124, 127–29, 135
Sowams, 1–2, 25, 38, 40, 147
Spanish colonists, 7, 8, 13, 19, 20n58, 24–25, 44, 121
Squanto, 24, 143. *See also* Tisquantum
Standish, Miles: and attack on Massachusetts, 4, 77, 90–97, 158, 165; as military leader, 59–63, 59n12, 133, 134n26,

137, 144, 155; trading voyages of, 69–71, 73, 76–79, 87, 101

Tisquantum: as captive, 24–25, 80n65, 112, 127, 143, 163; death of, 72; and epidemics, 26–27, 66, 136; as interpreter, 25–26, 37, 39–40, 59–60, 62–65, 70–71, 74, 147, 149, 151–52, 163; and Massasoit, 25–26, 64–66; rumors told by, 40, 63–66. *See also* captives: taken by Hunt
tobacco, 1, 11, 75, 109, 113, 117, 145, 152–53
Tokamahamon, 59, 152–53

Verrazzano, Giovanni da, 20, 121–24
Virginia: climate of, 32, 113; colony in, 6, 18, 34, 68–69, 111, 141; and Powhatans' attack, 12–13, 15, 116–17

Wampanoags: alliance with Plimoth, 4, 36–39, 44, 47, 64–65, 79, 84, 143–47, 151, 155, 163; hospitality of, 2, 4, 47, 79, 84, 149–55; illnesses of, 10, 27–29, 83, 105; language of, 47–48, 48n136; response to Europeans, 12, 16–17, 20, 22–24, 26, 36–37, 47; in the twenty-first century, 47–48. *See also* captives: taken by Hunt; captives: Wampanoag
weather: cold, 33, 73, 75–76, 78–79, 91, 106, 124, 136–37; drought, 99–101; hot, 113, 150; stormy, 60, 65, 93, 100–101, 136, 153–54
Wessagusset colonists: arrival of, 35, 66–70, 73, 128–29, 160; attack on the Massachusetts, 42, 88 by; departure of, 44, 96; as disorderly colony, 34–36, 57–58, 68–69, 88–89, 93, 164; food for, 35, 66–68, 73, 88, 93, 96, 162; living with the Massachusetts, 4, 35, 41, 93, 95, 97, 163; relations with the Massachusetts, 35, 42, 88–89, 128, 158–63; reports of New England from, 98; starvation of, 88–89, 160; suspicions of Massachusetts, 40, 90–91, 158–62; theft of corn by, 35, 41–42, 88–89, 91, 160
Weston, Thomas, 35, 66, 68–70, 73, 77, 84, 88, 91, 95–96
Winslow, Edward: as colonial agent, 17, 44; as colonial diplomat, 2–3, 17–19, 37–39, 79, 144, 147–52; cure of Massasoit, 1–5, 10, 79–84; early life in England of,